"*Emotion-Savvy Parenting* is an inspiring, paradigm-shifting book for traversing the beautifully rocky road of parenting. Rooted in science, full of wisdom, and entertaining throughout, Dr. Alissa Jerud has packed this book with powerful skills and memorable anecdotes to help parents manage their *own* emotions, thus radically transforming their parenting journeys for the better."

Eve Rodsky, *New York Times* best-selling author of *Fair Play*

"It's one thing to say you don't want unruly emotions in the driver's seat during the most challenging moments of parenting life, but it's hard to know where to begin. This book provides the roadmap. With engaging personal and clinical stories, practical tips, and a clear science-backed framework, Dr. Alissa Jerud equips parents to more confidently and enjoyably navigate the emotional tumults of parenting."

Yael Schonbrun, PhD, author of *Work, Parent, Thrive*

"*Emotion-Savvy Parenting* is a nonjudgmental, indispensable guide to peaceful, enjoyable parenting. Through research, relatable anecdotes, and her own professional experience, Dr. Alissa Jerud empowers parents to focus on controlling their own (rather than their children's) behavior. This must-read book provides all the practical, science-backed tools caregivers need to stay calm, loving, caring, and respectful – even in the midst of the most chaotic, emotionally charged moments."

Phyllis L. Fagell, LCPC, school counselor, and author of *Middle School Matters* and *Middle School Superpowers*

"*Emotion-Savvy Parenting* provides wise advice on how to be a better parent in today's chaotic world. Reading it, I couldn't help wishing this book had been written 20 years ago, when I started my journey as a parent. Powerful, practical, and a must-read for all adults who strive to positively impact children's lives."

Tal Ben-Shahar, PhD, founder of Happiness Studies Academy and *New York Times* best-selling author of *Happier*

"As a clinical psychologist who specializes in helping mothers cope with the many stresses of parenting, I couldn't wait to read Dr. Alissa Jerud's new book, *Emotion-Savvy Parenting*. Dr. Jerud's book highlights such an important premise: that parents need to focus less on changing their children's emotional responses (an impossible task, we can all agree) and focus instead on learning to manage their own. With warmth and candor, Dr. Jerud shares research-supported, user-friendly tools that parents can employ in the moment to help them cope more effectively with their frustration, respond to their children with more patience, and yes, even enjoy parenting more. I am so excited to recommend this book to my patients!"

Ilyse Dobrow DiMarco, PhD, licensed
clinical psychologist and author of *Mom Brain*

"Whatever the size of the emotional storms in your child, your family or yourself, Dr. Jerud can help you skillfully navigate these by focusing on changing what's yours to control and accepting what isn't."

Christopher Willard, PsyD, clinical psychologist
and author of *Growing Up Mindful* and *Raising Resilience*

"Dr. Alissa Jerud has broken new ground by weaving together her own personal experiences as a parent with a refreshingly clear set of instructions to give parents validation along with evidence-based tools to tackle the most common challenges of modern parenthood. *Emotion-Savvy Parenting* invites parents to first delve into our own experiences and vulnerabilities without falling into tactics that focus exclusively on "fixing" our kiddos. Dr. Jerud's approach is validating and compassionate and should be required reading for all parents and parents-to-be who would like a game plan to bring a more balanced approach to the wild ride of parenting!"

Dan Singley, PhD, licensed psychologist and
founding director of The Center for Men's Excellence

"In her new book, Dr. Alissa Jerud compassionately convinces parents to confront the frustrating, humbling – and simultaneously liberating – reality that learning to manage our *own* emotions is the key to weathering and calming our children's emotional storms. As the mom of 11 and 13 year old boys, I started using her practical strategies immediately, including last night when teen emotions ran high. Dr. Jerud is in the trenches with us, and her book is a must-read no matter the age of your child!"

Lori Mihalich-Levin, JD, CEO of Mindful Return
and author of *Back to Work After Baby*

Emotion-Savvy Parenting

Intense emotions – whether your own or your child's – can make it incredibly difficult to be the parent you want to be. This book is designed to help you become a more emotionally agile parent so you can better navigate whatever emotional storms you inevitably encounter.

Emotion-Savvy Parenting is an empowering, science-informed guide for breaking free of the hold that unwanted emotions so often have over parents. With compassion and wit, licensed clinical psychologist Dr. Alissa Jerud draws on decades of research to present a refreshing, theory-driven approach that encourages parents to focus on changing the only behaviors they truly have control over: their own. Rooted in highly effective, cognitive-behavioral strategies and a respectful, relationship-centered stance, her ART (Accept, Regulate, and Tolerate) framework enables parents to relate more skillfully to challenging emotions, model invaluable lessons, connect more deeply with their kids, and enjoy parenting more.

Packed with real-life examples and step-by-step techniques, this book supports parents of infants to teens in creating a more harmonious home by becoming their ideal, most emotionally adept selves. It also serves as a valuable resource for educators and mental health professionals seeking to help lighten the heavy load of parenthood.

Alissa Jerud, PhD, is a licensed clinical psychologist and clinical assistant professor at the University of Pennsylvania specializing in evidence-based treatments for anxiety and emotion regulation difficulties, including those that come with parenting.

Emotion-Savvy Parenting

A Shame-Free Guide to Navigating
Emotional Storms and Deepening
Connection

ALISSA JERUD, PhD

Routledge
Taylor & Francis Group

NEW YORK AND LONDON

Designed cover image: Getty Images

First published 2025
by Routledge
605 Third Avenue, New York, NY 10158

and by Routledge
4 Park Square, Milton Park, Abingdon, Oxon, OX14 4RN

Routledge is an imprint of the Taylor & Francis Group, an informa business

Library of Congress Cataloging-in-Publication Data
Names: Jerud, Alissa B., author.
Title: Emotion-savvy parenting : a shame-free guide to navigating
    emotional storms and deepening connection / Alissa Jerud.
Description: Abingdon, Oxon ; New York, NY : Routledge, 2025. |
    Includes bibliographical references and index. | Identifiers:
    LCCN 2024057584 (print) | LCCN 2024057585 (ebook) | ISBN
    9781032549712 (hardback) | ISBN 9781032544946 (paperback) |
    ISBN 9781003428343 (ebook)
Subjects: LCSH: Parents—Psychology. | Parent and child. | Child
    rearing. | Emotions.
Classification: LCC HQ755.8 .J475 2025 (print) | LCC HQ755.8
    (ebook) | DDC 155.6/46–dc23/eng/20250128
LC record available at https://lccn.loc.gov/2024057584
LC ebook record available at https://lccn.loc.gov/2024057585

ISBN: 978-1-032-54971-2 (hbk)
ISBN: 978-1-032-54494-6 (pbk)
ISBN: 978-1-003-42834-3 (ebk)

DOI: 10.4324/9781003428343

Typeset in Times New Roman
by Apex CoVantage, LLC

Access the Support Material: www.routledge.com/9781032544946

For Jackson Antonio Clark, who lives on in the acts of kindness his memory has inspired countless others to perform

And for Ayelet and Hillel, who light up my world and make me want to do better every day

Contents

Acknowledgments

No words could possibly convey the immense gratitude I feel for the many individuals who have helped make this book possible in one way or another. Although I have attempted to credit all those who have championed this book in the paragraphs that follow, I want to begin by thanking anyone I have inadvertently left out who has helped shape this book in some way. I also want to thank the parents I have known, both personally and professionally, who have shared their thoughts, feelings, and stories with me. I am eternally grateful for every single one of you.

Of course, special thanks go to my own loving parents for the countless ways in which they have shown up for me. Mom, thank you for helping me hone my craft as a writer long ago and for providing encouragement and support over the years and throughout this writing. Dad, I knew from an early age that I could paint the canvas of my life however I wished, and that was largely thanks to you.

To my siblings, Brett, Kim, and Todd, I have looked up to the three of you for as long as I can remember – literally and figuratively – and I am so grateful for your love and friendship. And to my sister-in-law, Tamar, thank you for always being there for me. I also want to thank the entire Jerud crew for welcoming me into your family with open arms so many years ago and for all of your support since then.

My deepest thanks go to my graduate school mentor, Dr. Lori Zoellner, for her generosity of time and spirit, not only while I was a student, but also to this day. Thank you for teaching me the value of persistence, for allowing me to forge me own, unique path, and for being such a motivating force in my life. And to my former lab mates and colleagues at the University of Washington, thank you for your camaraderie and collaboration.

I'd also like to express my sincere appreciation to Dr. Marsha Linehan and the entire team at the University of Washington's Behavioral Research and Therapy Clinics (BRTC), now known as the Marsha M. Linehan DBT Clinic. Thank you for the unparalleled training experiences you provided me, without which this book would not have been possible. And to Dr. Edna Foa and the many wonderful people at the University of Pennsylvania's Center for the Treatment and Study of Anxiety (CTSA), please know that I will forever be grateful for all I have learned from you.

To my friends who supported and advised me over the years, thank you. I am especially thankful for the many hours that Drs. Terri Bacow, Joel Minden, Shari Jager-Hyman, Natalia Garcia, and Laurie Zandberg generously gave to read and offer feedback on my writing. This book is better because of each of you.

Speaking of making this book better (and possible), I am incredibly grateful for the entire Routledge team, especially Sarah Gore, Julia Giordano, and Alice Maher. Your patience, kindness, and unwavering encouragement and support of this project have helped make this book a reality, and I can't thank you enough for that.

Last, but certainly not least, I want to express my deepest, most heartfelt thanks to my incredible husband, Elliot, and my amazing children, Ayelet and Hillel. Elliot, you believed in me even when I didn't and have been my sounding board from day one, as well as a constant source of levity and light. Ayelet and Hillel, the two of you bring so much love, joy, and beauty to my life, and I truly marvel at the remarkable people you have become. Thank you for allowing me to grow up alongside you and for loving me so fiercely, despite my many mistakes. I am beyond lucky to be your Ima.

Author's Note

The advice I share in *Emotion-Savvy Parenting* is informed by my own training and work as a clinical psychologist, as well as my own parenting experience. While the anecdotes that I've included from my own life are entirely true, the other scenarios are loosely based on stories told to me by others I have known either personally or professionally. I am indebted to these people for sharing their stories with me and have used composites and changed all identifying details, including names, to protect their privacy.

I am thrilled you are reading *Emotion-Savvy Parenting* and hope it helps you grow as much as I have while writing it. That said, please note that this book is not intended as a substitute for tailored advice from a trained professional. If you believe it might be helpful for you or your child to meet with a mental health provider, please see the Resources section in the support material for this book (www.routledge.com/9781032544946) for a list of organizations that may be able to point you in the right direction.

Foreword

It's no secret that parents often feel exhausted and overwhelmed by the enormous project of raising children. In 2024, the United States Surgeon General issued an official advisory on parental mental health and well-being, highlighting the need for better resources to help alleviate the emotional, financial, and logistical pressures involved in keeping small humans alive and well. After all, as Dr. Alissa Jerud aptly acknowledges in the opening pages of *Emotion-Savvy Parenting*, parenting really is the most challenging job in the world. And while our collective parenting burden is indeed greatly impacted by financial, systemic, and logistical stressors, it is the emotional challenge of parenting that is the particular focus of this wonderful book. And what a welcome and much-needed focus!

As a mother of two and a clinical psychologist who frequently works with other parents to help them manage the myriad of difficult emotions that come with parenting, I know how desperate you likely are for guidance in this area. Although there's no shortage of parenting advice these days, most of what's out there either focuses on helping parents change their kids' behaviors (often at the expense of the parent-child relationship) or prioritizes parent-child bonds (often at the expense of parents' own emotional well-being).

Dr. Jerud's approach, in contrast, addresses what parents most need: tools for managing their *own* emotions while also deepening connection as they navigate the very normal, often frustrating behaviors that we see in our children across the age spectrum. This blend is exactly what stressed-out parents have been missing and what they need. A seasoned clinical psychologist, clinical assistant professor, and mother of two, Dr. Jerud very much understands that we adults – despite being "grownups" – do not always have all the skills we need to regulate our own emotions (after all these are learned and taught), let alone to help our children manage their ever-changing feelings. Even those of us who consider ourselves emotionally intelligent know how impossible it can seem at times to skillfully navigate the strong emotions that show up in us while trying to raise the energetic, easily dysregulated, and occasionally (or frequently) obstinate youngsters with whom we live. But here's the good news: No matter your current emotional quotient, it's never too late to become a more emotionally savvy parent. In fact, by picking up this book, you're already well on your way. Indeed, if you've been searching for a resource to help you better manage the anger, anxiety, frustration, sadness, guilt, and more that we all feel as parents, keep reading! This is the book for you.

Get ready to feel supported and empowered by Dr. Jerud, who brings the very concepts and tools she uses in her clinical work out of the office and into this fabulous book, making them come alive in a clear and accessible way. Although I'll leave it to her to do the teaching, all you need to know for now is that you are about to learn a host of science-backed skills that she has adapted from the most robust, evidence-based treatments currently available in our field to help you become the parent and role model you want to be.

Lest you think you might be in for some boring and convoluted academic prose, prepare instead to be entertained and to not want to put down this book. Dr. Jerud explains her approach and the strategies that comprise it with masterful writing, vivid examples from the trenches, and helpful figures and tables that you can refer to again and again in your most challenging parenting moments. Moreover, the skills you will learn are presented in a brilliant, innovative, and highly effective framework that will help you accept, regulate, and tolerate your and your children's emotions, no matter the emotional temperature within your home.

In short, this book is a much-needed, refreshing resource that speaks to the needs of struggling parents (also known as ALL of us at some point or another). Invigorating in its honesty and transparency, as well as in its emphasis on progress over perfection, this is the book I wish I had when I was a new parent and one I will continue to refer to as my now tween and teen grow. After all, the gems in this book apply across the age span and are not limited to any one developmental stage, making it a truly essential resource for parents. Thus, whatever your current struggles happen to be, if you are a parent or caregiver who, like me, has been seeking a "playbook" for parenting that can give you science-informed strategies to help you up your game and keep your cool, look no further! Most of all, in reading this book, prepare to feel seen and transformed for the better. While your child will certainly and undoubtedly benefit from what you read here, YOU as a parent (and human) will be the ultimate winner.

Terri Bacow, PhD
Author of *Goodbye, Anxiety: A Guided Journal
for Overcoming Worry*

Introduction

"I hate that I get so frustrated and angry with my kids!
I want to enjoy my time with them but so rarely do.
They're just so wild! I feel stuck and desperately wish
I knew what I could do to create a warmer, more peaceful home."

Although not everyone has the courage to share their parenting woes so openly, I happen to hear comments like this all the time from loved ones, friends, and patients alike. And the truth is, we all feel this way sometimes – myself included. Though soul-crushing, these moments of apparent defeat can also be transformational. To illustrate, let me take you back a few years ago to one of my own, life-altering low points as a parent.

****

Like a tuning fork, my friend's words reverberated in my mind as I sat at the memorial service for her two-year-old son: Time with her sweet boy had been a gift, not a given. There she was, my grief-stricken friend who would have given anything to have one more day with her beloved child. And there I was, harboring the dread that I had felt on so many days prior when thinking about spending time with mine. A wave of guilt washed over me as I contemplated this harsh reality and realized how imperceptive I had been.

As a mom of two young kids, I was struggling to be the parent I wanted to be. My then four-year-old daughter had become increasingly defiant since the birth of her baby brother, and I was feeling outmatched, inept, and completely overwhelmed. Certain that I would only make it out of

DOI: 10.4324/9781003428343-1

the woods if I could get my daughter to become more compliant, I tried tactic after tactic in search of one that would convince her to change. Regrettably, however, the harder I fought to control my daughter's behavior, the more distant and wilder she became and the more unhinged and exasperated I grew.

Although I was truly trying my best, I had for months been oblivious to the role I was playing in this frustrating cycle. Yet, as I watched my friend finish delivering a heart-wrenching eulogy for her son, it all became painfully clear to me that it wasn't my daughter who needed to change. Reflecting on my own behavior, I realized how unhelpful my understandably angry reactions had been. Not only was my anger burning me out, but it was also likely confirming my daughter's false belief that I loved her brother more than I loved her, thus leading her to act out even more. With tears streaming down my cheeks, I considered the fragility of life and how I had inadvertently taken my daughter's for granted, assuming that if I failed to convey my deep love for her one day, I'd always have the next day to fall back on. My tiny girl wasn't the problem – my approach was. And somehow or other, I needed to change course and find a way to be kinder and more compassionate toward both of us. I left the service and returned home, determined to approach each day with my daughter as though it could be our last.

****

Fast forward seven years to the present. Although my daughter's behavior has certainly improved, she remains a strong-willed and spirited kid. Plus, her sometimes sidekick, sometimes archenemy (my son) is now able to create his own whirlwind of chaos as well. In other words, my kids haven't made life all that much easier for me. Critically, however, pivoting away from trying to tame my daughter (and eventually my son, too) has made a world of difference. By focusing instead on quieting my own emotional reactivity, I have managed to cool the frayed ends of my once completely frazzled self and now feel much more competent and able to handle whatever my kids throw my way. Even better? I enjoy parenting so much more now and have a stronger relationship with my kids than ever before.

That said, as much as I wish I could say that I became a calmer, more loving mom overnight, behavior change almost never occurs that quickly – not for me or anyone else. Whether we are trying to give up sugar, coffee, alcohol, nail biting, perfectionism, or yelling at our kids, breaking our habitual, reflexive ways of moving through the world is remarkably challenging.

What's more, even when we do manage to change our ways, backslides are bound to happen for most of us. Indeed, it has taken a while for me to get to this calmer, less reactive place, and I certainly still have work to do.

Let's Be Real (and Hopeful)

My hope in writing this book is to help you get unstuck from whatever ruts you keep falling into as a parent, while also giving you the tools you need to pave a more scenic and peaceful route for your parenting journey. Having said that, in the interest of self-disclosure, let it be known that I do not consider myself to be a parenting expert. I should also probably note that – like the individuals I see in my work as a clinical psychologist – I, too, have moments where I allow powerful emotions to overtake me. And like you, I am also a parent who struggles at times (even still) to show up as I'd like with my kids. To claim otherwise would be to lie; unless, of course, I wasn't actually a living, breathing human. Indeed, when it comes to navigating the emotional roller coaster of life in general – and parenting in particular – the truth is we're all novices stumbling to varying extents, regardless of our age or title.

Be that as it may, I am incredibly grateful for my training as a clinical psychologist as it has enabled me to mostly break free of the hold that emotions, mine and those of others, used to have over me. It's also what inspired me to create the unique, relationship-centric approach I call Emotion-Savvy Parenting, forever altering my experience as a parent (and person) for the better. No, I am not a natural when it comes to navigating emotions, nor am I a mom who parents at all times with ease. However, I have benefited tremendously from living and breathing the perspectives and tools shared throughout this book on a daily basis, both in and out of the office, and I have had the honor and privilege of seeing these improve the lives of countless other parents I've worked with as well. My hope is that this book will do the same for you.

Is This Book for You?

If you are someone who struggles to be the parent you want to be in the face of your own intense emotions (i.e., every parent I have ever met), then this book is absolutely for you. That said, I realize you might be wondering whether a professional who sometimes screws up with her own kids can really give you the parenting help you're needing. And my answer? That depends.

If you are looking for a flawless parent who has the most well-behaved children on this planet to expertly shame you into becoming someone you aren't, then – if you haven't realized this already – you're reading the wrong book. If, on the other hand, you are looking for a non-judgmental guide who (like most parents) sometimes struggles to parent effectively but is trying her best to use the most up-to-date, evidence-based practices in order to do right by her kids, then keep reading.

Whether you are a parent of one, two, three, four, or more kids, I get how unfathomably hard this gig is that you've got going. As you read this, maybe you're drinking from a bottle of wine and wishing you could crawl into a hole and disappear for a few hours, days, or even weeks. Or maybe you're imagining teleporting back to your glory days before you had kids. You know, the days when you actually showered on a daily basis and could spend your weekends binge-watching your favorite shows or doing whatever you wanted to do. Alternatively, you may be dreaming of hopping on a plane and taking a luxurious, all-inclusive spa vacation where there are no Legos to step on, no fights to break up, and no boogers to wipe off your arm. If nothing else, wouldn't it be nice to just call out sick for the day? Whatever your fantasy happens to be, believe me, I get it.

Your kids are the center of your world and you love them more than anything. At the same time, being with them can be unimaginably taxing and sometimes downright infuriating. On some days, it's the graveyard of uncapped markers coupled with the constant soundtrack of increasingly louder screeches that gets to you. On other days, it's watching in horror from across the room as your eldest clobbers your toddler – yet again – before you can intervene that throws you over the edge. From there, things become a blur. The adoration you felt just moments prior becomes a distant memory as your heart pounds and your temperature seems to kick up 100 degrees. Suddenly, a voice you barely recognize screams out in a last-ditch attempt to regain control and put an end to the chaos. All eyes turn to you, revealing the heartbroken souls behind them or the emboldened spirits ready to up the ante. A part of you wants to make amends or call for a truce, yet you are too lost in the haze of emotions that has descended upon you to do anything but fan the flames. Words that you swore you would never say to your kids tumble from your mouth and you stomp away, praying your kids don't retaliate by destroying the room in your absence.

Sound familiar? If so, welcome to the club. While I don't know the details of your life, I know all too well the overwhelming feelings of anger, inadequacy, hopelessness, shame, sadness, and resentment that you likely feel on a regular, if not daily, basis. And I know from personal experience how difficult it can be to show up as the calm, loving, and capable leader you want to be when you are practically bursting with any one (or more) of these emotions. In these moments, the pull to yell at and criticize your kids in an attempt to control their intractable feelings and behaviors can seem almost insurmountable. One too many days like this may have even left you wondering whether the rest of your parenting years are doomed to be laden with these all-consuming negative emotions that lead you to act in ways that belie your love for your kids, thus leaving you feeling even more inept and defeated.

Thankfully, you can rest assured that this does not need to be the case at all. Although even the most skillful parents among us will flounder and make mistakes here and there, as I explain in the coming pages, we can all minimize the pain we inflict upon ourselves – as well as the collateral damage we cause – by becoming better at regulating our *own* emotions and by striving to treat our kids with unconditional love and respect. Hence, the reason I wrote this book.

How Emotion-Savvy Parenting Can Help

Those of you who are familiar with the parenting philosophy known as "gentle parenting" will readily recognize elements of this in Emotion-Savvy Parenting. In fact, my approach technically falls under the larger umbrella of gentle parenting methods. Yet, although I was certainly inspired by many of the tenets of gentle parenting, I prefer to think of my approach as an offshoot of the science-informed strategies I use in my clinical work more than anything else. Before explaining why, let me first tell you a bit about my work as a therapist, as well as how I've adapted this work for parents, specifically.

As an expert in cognitive-behavioral therapy (CBT), I specialize in exposure therapy for anxiety-related disorders (Abramowitz et al., 2019) and Dialectical Behavior Therapy (DBT) skills training for emotion regulation difficulties (Linehan, 2015). Like all forms of CBT, both treatments aim to help individuals develop new, more skillful relationships with painful or unwanted emotions, while also modifying the unhelpful thoughts and behaviors that fuel these feelings. Notably, these short-term forms of psychotherapy are supported by large bodies of research and have helped countless individuals all over the world live more effective, emotionally agile lives.

At the heart of these therapies is the powerful notion that we can experience intense or painful emotions *and* still choose to comport ourselves in ways that are effective and consistent with our values. In other words, we don't have to let our emotions call the shots. Instead, we can be the people we aspire to be no matter the circumstances.

Of course, this stands in stark contrast to the prevailing and completely understandable belief that if we want to feel and do better as parents, we just need to find the right scripts and tricks to get our kids to change. Yet, as I realized during the memorial service for my friend's son, the doctrine of CBT applies every bit as much to parenting as to anything else. No, we don't have to wait for our kids to shape up for us to be the parents we want to be. Instead, when equipped with skills, we can choose to show up as the best version of ourselves no matter what chaos is brewing in or around us. After all, as discussed in later chapters, our kids are going to act in ways that push our buttons, no matter which parenting methods we follow. Accordingly, rather than offer hacks for getting kids to "listen" or behave better, I aim to help parents see that the secret to a more harmonious home rests within us, not within our children.

While I do believe that a gentle parenting style is what's best for kids, not everyone does. Indeed, though I intend in the coming chapters to refute some of the arguments that have been lodged against gentle parenting, let's just say that criticism abounds. However, it's hard to argue with the countless scientific studies supporting the skills and ways of being that make up Emotion-Savvy Parenting. In the words of Dr. Susan David, Harvard psychologist and author of the enormously successful book, *Emotional Agility*: "Discomfort is the price of admission to a meaningful life" (David, 2016). In other words, if we want to have lives that we experience as worth living, we need to develop the ability to allow in and roll with the uncomfortable emotions that are guaranteed to tag along for the ride. And for reasons I'll get into later, nowhere is this more true than in parenting. Thus, as far as I'm concerned, we might as well choose to parent in a way that helps us become our ideal, most emotionally adept selves – if not for our kids, then at least for us.

As one parent recently shared with me, embracing the ideas and strategies shared in this book "feels liberating." I hear variations of this all the time and feel the same way myself. Sure, it would be nice, at least in theory, if we could wave a magic wand and never have to feel unwanted emotions again. Yet, since we can't get rid of these feelings altogether, why not learn to live more skillfully with them and connect more deeply with our kids in the process? This book is written to help you do just that.

How to Get the Most Out of This Book

Collectively, I refer to the strategies presented in this book as the ART and Science of Emotions or simply the ART Tools, with ART standing for Accept, Regulate, and Tolerate. More specifically, I present a set of skills for accepting emotions, a set of skills for regulating emotions, and a set of skills for tolerating emotions. These skills will likely sound familiar for those who have experience with exposure therapy and/or DBT (the two forms of CBT that I mentioned previously), as well as for those who have experience with Acceptance and Commitment Therapy (ACT; Hayes et al., 2016). What makes my framework unique is that I have adapted core concepts and strategies from these evidence-based treatments for parents, specifically, and have blended these with fundamental principles of gentle parenting to help you parent more effectively.

Notably, although the three different types of ART Tools I present are distinct, each set of skills complements the others. I therefore recommend reading the book from cover to cover in order to get the best picture of when, how, and why to use these tools, although you can certainly jump around if a section or chapter seems most relevant for you right now.

In Part 1, I explain how accepting, regulating, and tolerating our own emotions can help make the incredibly challenging task of raising human beings much more meaningful and rewarding. Specifically, in Chapter 1, I discuss the importance of accepting where we currently are as parents (mistakes and all) while also aiming to change the behaviors of ours that aren't serving us well. Chapter 2 builds on these ideas, offering a refreshing and uplifting perspective on parenting that frees us from the frustrating quest of trying to get our kids to change so we can instead focus on changing the things we actually can control. And just maybe, we might be pleasantly surprised to discover that modifying our own behaviors often (though not always) brings about positive changes in our children as well.

Next, in Part 2, I dive into the skills that make up the ART Tools and bring in many examples from my own life and the lives of others to illustrate how these skills can help you better accept, regulate, and tolerate the emotions you encounter as a parent. Chapter 3 focuses on acceptance and explains how mindfulness practice can help us more fully accept ourselves and our kids, challenging emotions and all. Chapter 4 is about regulating our emotions, which involves understanding the many components that make up emotional storms, as well as specific skills to target each of these, thus reducing the likelihood that storms will hit or intensify if they do. Last in this section, Chapter 5 consists of a set of distress tolerance skills to help you survive whatever emotional storms do come your way so you can show up as the parent you hope to be, no matter how intense the storms get. Of note, the skills presented in each of these three chapters are ones you can practice anytime, anywhere, whether with your kids or not. And of course, the more you practice using these skills, the more you will gain from them.

Finally, in Part 3, I provide actionable tips for accepting, regulating, and tolerating our own emotions, as well as our children's, in our messy, everyday lives. In Chapter 6, I give ART-informed suggestions for making the most of more peaceful moments with our kids. Then, in Chapter 7, I offer a collection of ART-based pointers for moments when your kids, you, or all involved are emotionally flooded or overwhelmed. And given that we are all guaranteed to make mistakes no matter how skilled we become at utilizing the ART Tools, Chapter 8 includes evidence-based techniques for getting back on track when our emotions get the best of us, as well as science-informed strategies for overcoming common obstacles to becoming a more emotionally savvy parent.

One additional note: I encourage you to try using all of the skills in this book more than once, even if they initially seem strange, unnatural, or uncomfortable. As a reminder, every skill I describe in this book has a great deal of evidence supporting its effectiveness. Thus, it's worth giving each of these a shot. That said, you may find some skills more helpful than others and may come to rely on these favorites as your go-to tools. This is perfectly fine and is something that I do myself. However, I suggest returning to the skills that appeal to you the least from time to time as these may resonate with you more as you and your children grow and new challenges arise. At the end of the day, given that parenting is quite possibly the hardest job on the planet, why not stock your toolkit with as many potentially useful tools as possible?

References

Abramowitz, J. S., Deacon, B. J., & Whiteside, S. P. H. (2019). *Exposure therapy for anxiety: Principles and practice* (2nd ed.). The Guilford Press.

David, S. (2016). *Emotional agility: Get unstuck, embrace change, and thrive in work and life*. Avery/Penguin Random House.

Hayes, S. C., Strosahl, K. D., & Wilson, K. G. (2016). *Acceptance and commitment therapy: The process and practice of mindful change* (2nd ed.). The Guilford Press.

Linehan, M. M. (2015). *DBT skills training manual* (2nd ed.). The Guilford Press.

Part 1
The Most Challenging Job in the World

Everyone Makes Mistakes

1

Welcome to the Imperfect Parenting Club

It was a hot and humid day in the unusually stressful summer of 2020, three years after the aha moment I mentioned in the Introduction, and I was feeling beyond exhausted. For months, I had been juggling two full-time jobs due to the pandemic – caring for my two young children during the day and seeing a full caseload of patients at night – and I was desperate for a break. Ignoring the oppressive conditions outside, I decided to take my kids and dog to a nearby state park to get some exercise and escape the mess of clutter and toys covering just about every inch of our house.

Although my kids usually love being outside, it was clear from the moment that we got to the park that this was not going to be a joyous outing for any of us. My then seven-year-old, who had insisted on wearing leggings, a heavy t-shirt, and rain boots despite the weather, complained that she was sticky and sweaty almost immediately after stepping out of the car. And my son, who was three years old at the time and determined to venture off on his own, became enraged when I let him know I couldn't allow him to do so. At first, I considered hopping back into the car and driving us all home. However, when I realized doing so would mean spending yet another long day inside the walls of our overcrowded home, I decided to validate my kids' distress while letting them know that it wouldn't be time to leave for another hour or two.

Not too long after making this announcement, my kids found a large and enticing puddle of mud that they couldn't wait to explore. With brightened moods, they reached for sticks and leaves to poke at and stir up the mud and

DOI: 10.4324/9781003428343-3

created all sorts of gooey concoctions to share with each other. Relieved that our outing wasn't going to be a total flop, I sat down a few feet away with our dog in my lap and marveled at the sweet play unfolding in front of me, oblivious to how quickly things would unravel from there.

Minutes later, my son accidentally bumped into my daughter, making her stumble into the thick mud in front of her. Angry that her yellow rain boots were now coated on both the inside and outside with mud, my daughter quickly regained her balance and shoved her brother with all her might, causing him to fall face-first into the puddle. Covered from head to toe in mud, my son screamed and cried as I picked him up and began to take off his clothes while my daughter giggled uncomfortably in the background. Meanwhile, judgment after judgment raced through my mind as I glared at my daughter, who could clearly see how upset I was with her. *Why did she have to push him into the mud? She should have known better! How could she be so mean? There was no need for her to get so upset!*

Trying to stay calm, I decided to shift my attention away from these thoughts and to instead focus on prying each item off as carefully as possible from my son's body, only to realize that the smell coming from his clothes was too offensive to just be mud. Now aware that an animal or two had likely visited the puddle before us, I turned to see that my daughter had taken off her boots and wiped them all over our dog's leash and wavy coat of white fur. Cue additional judgments and a surge of blood coursing through my veins. *What was she thinking? Why is she being so difficult? Why can't she give me a break?*

Disgusted and fuming inside, I put on my backpack, picked up my son, and began to inch back to the car, my arms overflowing with muddy shoes, boots, and clothes, as well as my son's scooter and my dog's leash. Barefoot, my daughter trailed behind me on her scooter at an even more glacial pace than mine, complaining the whole while about how hot and sweaty she was. My anger too intense to empathize with her in the moment, I brusquely acknowledged her discomfort and besought her help carrying the heap of items in my hands. Begrudgingly, she agreed to take both scooters and, after what seemed like hours of trudging along the trail, we finally made it back to our car, which was now burning up from having sat in the sun for so long.

What exactly happened next, I'm not sure: I was too flooded to fully encode the moment. However, as we piled into the car, both kids whining about being hot, muddy, and hungry, I can say with confidence that I was not at my best. Although I can't say for certain which harsh words were uttered or how many icy glares were given, I know that I made it abundantly clear, with words and body language alone, just how furious I was. Emotionally hijacked, this outward expression of anger wasn't entirely volitional. Nevertheless, I do remember hoping that this rare and intense emotional display might bring about more compliance from my kids that day. If nothing else, maybe I'd get a few minutes of peace and quiet so I could calm down and recharge?

Oh, how wrong I was. Rather than make them cower in their seats, my anger and attempts to rein in my kids only added fuel to the fire, intensifying their grumblings and willfulness. Once everyone was buckled in, I turned on some calming music and demanded (again, I was not at my finest) a few moments of silence so I could listen to the melody and breathe along with it. Instead, my kids responded with ear-splitting screams. Heart pounding and face flushed, I reached for the car's volume dial and quickly flicked my wrist to adjust it. Music blared from the speakers, causing all three of us to jump in our seats and cry out in pain. Shaken and feeling like the worst parent in the world, I immediately turned the volume down to a more appropriate level and pulled over to regroup before starting to drive again.

Seconds after getting back on the road, the screaming started again, somehow this time even louder than before. Zipping my lips, I decided to try to ignore the noise and hope my kids would get tired of shouting at some point.

Unfortunately, it turns out my kids have an uncanny ability to scream at the top of their lungs for prolonged periods of time, especially in the face of injustice. Emboldened by the obvious effect their screaming was having on me, my daughter started yelling out the words written on every street sign we passed while my son, in turn, echoed each word as loudly as he could. With tears welling up in my eyes and the thought *Why can't they just shut up already?!?!* roaring in my head, I was nanoseconds away from shouting STOP! and slamming my foot on the car's break.

And then it hit me. Of course they weren't stopping. As is almost always the case, my attempts to control the situation were making all of us, especially me, feel woefully out of control. Likewise, my anger was making my kids every bit as dysregulated as I was. I therefore had two choices: I could either continue rebuking my kids in my head, thereby prolonging my misery (as well as theirs), or I could stop fighting my kids and partner with them instead. Opting for the latter, I started hollering the words on the signs we passed along with my daughter: "95 SOUTH! SPEED LIMIT 65 MILES PER HOUR! PERSONAL INJURY LAWYER! ROAD WORK AHEAD!" And so on. Within seconds, my anger melted away and I found myself cracking up at how much fun I was having with the little people I had been so livid with just moments earlier. We screamed and laughed together the entire ride and, once home, I apologized for my actions, bathed us all, and put on a movie for the kids so I could take some time to unwind and reflect on how I had ended up in such a precarious state.

We All Lose It Sometimes

As an expert in emotion regulation, I have a number of evidence-based strategies at my disposal to help me *not* lose it with my kids, so it's easy for me to beat myself up when I do. In these moments, my inner critic usually says the very same things I was thinking about my daughter earlier that day: *What was I thinking? I should know better! How could I be so mean?* Naturally, this was one of those days. I felt ashamed and couldn't believe I had blown it – yet again. But as I sat in a pool of my own tears, I caught myself. Just as castigating my kids hadn't been effective, doing the same to myself wasn't helpful either. I am human, after all, and my expertise doesn't change that. No matter how many skills I have in my arsenal, I will inevitably make mistakes, just as you and every other parent on this planet will.

Allowing this truth to sink in for a bit enabled me to move past the overwhelming level of shame I had been feeling so I could begin to dissect what had happened that day and strategize how I might do better in the future. Yes, my daughter had pushed my son into a putrid puddle of who-knows-what, and I had every right to be upset about this. That said, acting on my anger hadn't helped the situation at all. Instead, my angry urges had clouded my judgment, leading me to fight reality rather than accept and roll with it (even if not liking it) – as strong, uncomfortable emotions often do. In short, I had stumbled into one of the most deceptive, easy-to-fall-for traps we all encounter as parents, or people for that matter. It's the trap we find ourselves in when we try to change others (rather than ourselves), and is likely not only the same trap you keep falling for, too, but also the very reason you picked up this book in the first place. More on this to come.

The Road Less Traveled

At first glance, this focus on ourselves and our own behaviors may seem counterintuitive. If only our kids would stop whining, throwing tantrums, fighting, etc., life would be so much easier and we wouldn't lose our cool so much, right? Having said that, I've come to think of tactics used to eradicate our children's challenging behaviors as pseudo-elixirs for the struggles we face as parents. The reason? These tactics, while sometimes effective in the short term, provide little relief in the long run and often come with unfortunate, unintended costs.

To elucidate, I like to think of our children's emotions like the weather – frequently fluctuating, often with little warning. Likewise, our emotions also come and go, occasionally catching us off guard and unprepared. Yet, in contrast to our children, who lack the cognitive maturity needed to modulate the storms that brew within them, we are neurologically capable of calming (and even preventing) our own emotional storms.

With this in mind, the question becomes how to best navigate the challenging emotions that arise not only within us but also within our kids. While common parenting lore suggests that the key to becoming a happier parent is to figure out how to control and quiet our children's challenging emotions and behaviors (thus removing the main trigger for our own), this approach is, ironically, what tends to leave us feeling angry, frustrated, and inadequate as it can easily set us up for failure. Indeed, even when we find ways to temporarily halt our children's emotional outbursts or extinguish their behavioral manifestations, the underlying feelings don't just magically disappear. Instead, these feelings tend to swell and remain bottled up inside our kids until they eventually get released in some other way that we are likely to find equally aggravating, if not more so.

Accordingly, rather than order or wish away these emotional surges and their corresponding behaviors, we are much better off learning to live with and respond effectively to them. Indeed, when we accept our children's storms as inevitable and out of their control, we find ourselves better able to thwart and dial down our own, thus avoiding the epic cyclones that can form when our children's storms collide with ours. Moreover, when we refrain from exploding and instead serve as a calming force for our kids, we make it easier for them to regain their composure, too.

Believe me, I realize this is much easier said than done. That said, if we can learn to respond skillfully to the ever-changing emotions within and around us – as I hope to help you do in this book – then we will finally have the most important key needed for unlocking a more peaceful, loving, and connected home.

To be sure, the goings-on in my own abode often look, feel, and sound anything but calm and harmonious. And yet, despite the chaos and bickering that often ensues, pivoting away from trying to tame my two strong-willed kids has made parenting so much more bearable (and enjoyable) for me. Indeed, when I am able to focus on quieting my own emotional reactivity (rather than my kids'), I end up feeling so much more competent and capable of handling whatever my kids throw my way. That said, even though I *know* trying to control my kids will almost invariably result in all of us feeling more out of control, I still struggle at times – particularly when feeling angry – to refrain from acting on these urges.

And this is the trap I mentioned earlier. It's as though we are in quicksand: The more we try to fight and control our kids, the faster we sink. Accordingly, I have come to think of these moments when we feel on the verge of exploding and using force to meet our needs as critical choice points in our parenting journeys. We can either give in to our angry urges to control and lash out or we can notice these urges and choose to act calmly and empathically instead while confidently setting and holding needed limits. Fortunately, each time we choose the latter over the former, we strengthen the connections in our brains that wire for this new way of responding, thus making it more likely that we'll take a higher, more loving road the next time we're feeling triggered. Indeed, as is the case when trying to acquire any new skill, mastery can only come with repeated practice.

It's worth noting, however, that mastery is not the same as perfection. Just as the greatest basketball players continue to miss shots at the peak of their careers despite years of training, even the most emotionally adept parents occasionally veer from the path of equanimity when with their kids, regardless of how many times they've practiced maintaining their composure in the past. That's not a reason to stop practicing, however.

What to Expect

In the coming chapters, you will find a compelling, science-informed case and guide for embarking on a more conscious, confident, and compassionate parenting journey, as well as a map for returning to this new, unconventional path when you find yourself straying from it. As you read, please keep in mind that my goal in writing this book is to help you feel empowered by presenting an alternative approach to parenting that makes it easier for everyone involved – not just when emotions are running high, but anytime you are with your kids. Thus, if at any point you find yourself feeling overwhelmed by the prospect of making such a radical transformation, please be gentle with yourself. There is no need to change overnight, and you are doing the best you can with the tools you currently have. In fact, although this book is packed with helpful skills for better managing your emotions, it will likely take time and lots of trial and error before you feel confident in your ability to consistently and effectively regulate your emotions when with your kids. And as I said before, we *all* lose it at times. So, don't forget to give yourself the same grace when you mess up that I encourage giving to your kids.

None of us will ever be perfect as parents, and it's okay to stumble when we can't find our footing. In fact, I can almost guarantee you will fall, again and again, just as I have. It's for this reason that I recommend keeping this book on your nightstand or in a place where you can easily refer back to it so you can use it to help you reset and get back on track, when needed. If we work together in this way, my words serving as a dependable coach for you from here on, I truly believe we can pave the way for a very different, gentler reality for us, our children, and even society as a whole. If nothing else, it is my sincere hope that this book will give you the tools you need to lighten the heavy load of parenthood, thus enabling you to better appreciate the gift of time you have with your children. And so, without further ado, I invite you to turn the page and join me in creating your own next chapter.

Feeling Frazzled and Disconnected?

2

It Doesn't Have to Be This Way

In the world of parenting, there are at least two things most parents can agree on: 1) we love our children immensely and 2) parenting is hard – really hard. Although other seasoned parents may warn us ahead of time that we are in for a rocky, sleep-deprived ride, many of us dismiss these cautionary tales as ones that almost certainly won't apply to us. It's not that we are trying to fool ourselves, it's just that we are genuinely confident that our parenting journeys will be different. We will be the hip, fun, always-put-together parents whose well-mannered, loving kids admire and happily obey us at all times. Sound familiar?

Given that you are reading this book, I'm guessing that at some point over the past few days, weeks, months, or years, you made the unfortunate discovery that parenting isn't as exhausting, demanding, and maddening as others forewarned; it's even more so. No matter how highly skilled you are in other areas of your life, you likely find yourself feeling woefully ill-equipped at times to raise another human, let alone multiple ones at once. If so, please take comfort in knowing that I have yet to meet a parent for whom this hasn't been the case.

In fact, whether you are the CEO of a Fortune 500 company, a teacher, a stay-at-home parent, or a clinical psychologist like me, being a parent is likely the most difficult job you will ever have. Although you may be able to command a courtroom or an important meeting with ease, when it comes to parenting, there is a good chance that you feel as though you are floundering more than you would like. Or, if we are being honest, you likely *are*

DOI: 10.4324/9781003428343-4

floundering at times; not because you are a bad parent, but once again, just because parenting is so unbelievably hard.

Sure, parenting can be incredibly rewarding and even thrilling at times, and that's one of the reasons why I chose to write this book: to help others deepen the sense of fulfillment and joy they find in parenting. Yet, for many of us, these blissful snippets will never fully drown out the disappointment we feel when confronted with the fact that, on the whole, being a parent is much more overwhelming and much less glamorous than we'd hoped it would be. After all, as parents, we are on call 24/7 and are expected to carry an unwieldy load of tasks and responsibilities, no matter what other challenges we have on our plates. This alone would be enough to drain us of just about every ounce of energy we have. In addition, we spend a good chunk of our time with children who, due in large part to the nature of their developing brains, engage in a myriad of behaviors that can be annoying and infuriating for even the most cool, calm, and collected among us, thus further depleting our low reserves.

Although you can probably spout off an even lengthier list in mere seconds, here are just some of the things that kids sometimes do that tend to rattle parents:

- hit, kick, push, and bite;
- take toys from siblings and other kids;
- stall during transitions (especially when leaving the house and at bedtime);
- make messes of gargantuan proportions;
- whine, cry, scream, and have tantrums;
- ignore or defy instructions or requests;
- say or shout socially unacceptable things (e.g., "I hate you!" or my favorite to date, "Eww, you smell like vagina!"); and
- act in other socially unacceptable ways (e.g., fall out of chairs; eat a bowl of Spaghetti-O's with fingers – one ring at a time).

What's more, many of us are responsible for taking care of not just one, but multiple children, thus increasing the likelihood of being bombarded with these challenging behaviors. For instance, even though I only have two children, there have certainly been days on which both kids have managed to emit every single one of the behaviors listed earlier, either in succession or simultaneously. As you can imagine (or maybe already know), this kind of dynamic can quickly turn quality family time into a prolonged game of whack-a-mole, minus any of the fun. Indeed, it's in situations like these that I struggle the most.

Blame It on Development

No matter how rattled we might feel by the things our kids do and say, it is essential to understand that the types of behaviors discussed here are actually to be expected given what we know about brain development. Without going into too much detail, it's worth noting that the areas of our brains that allow us to feel and act on our emotions and impulses develop well before the "thinking" part of our brains, known as the executive center (or more formally, the prefrontal cortex). Critically, although the executive center does not fully develop until the age of 25 (Casey et al., 2008), it is needed in order to inhibit the unhelpful action urges that sometimes accompany intense emotions. Yet, because it is the last part of our brains to develop, during childhood, the executive center is no match for our brain's more primitive parts.

This means that when our children are feeling powerful emotions, their executive centers may not be able to put the brakes on their impulses. Thus, no matter how poised and mature our children may otherwise seem, when strong emotions are on board, they are likely to engage in messy, developmentally expected but socially inappropriate behaviors. Stated another way, when kids "misbehave," test limits, throw tantrums, or do things that they *know* they are not supposed to do or that they usually do not do, they are not trying to be defiant, manipulative, or mean. Instead, they are letting us know (in the best way they can) that their executive centers have been hijacked and that they need help in order to regain their footing.

According to Dr. Ross Greene, author of *Raising Human Beings* and *The Explosive Child* (Greene, 2016, 2021), the function of children's challenging behaviors is to communicate a current lack of the skills required in order to adhere to certain rules or conventions. Or, as he puts it, "kids do well when they can." Of note, this is different from the prevailing belief that acting-out behaviors function as a way to meet certain needs. Whereas the latter belief suggests that misbehavior "works" for children in some way (e.g., they get what they want), the former suggests that these behaviors are a sign something *isn't* working for them. This distinction is key because it can greatly influence how we respond to these behaviors. If we believe kids are benefitting from their challenging behaviors, then we will likely try to convey through our response that these behaviors are no longer going to work for them. For instance, we may punish kids when they emit these behaviors or reward them when they engage in a preferred behavior. By contrast, if we believe our kids' challenging behaviors function to inform us that their executive centers have momentarily been overthrown, then we are much less likely to worry about reinforcing misbehavior and much more likely to provide the support our children need in order to return their executive centers to power.

Unintended Consequences

Regrettably, the responses that most of us have to these cries for help are too often anything but helpful. As noted previously, when feeling irked by our children's behaviors, it's normal to want to fall apart ourselves and tighten the grip we have on our kids, especially if we view these behaviors as willful or falling outside the realm of healthy development or what's socially acceptable. We may try distracting, cajoling, bribing, yelling, threatening, or punishing our kids in an attempt to get back some semblance of control and put an end to the behaviors that are upsetting us so much. Alternatively, we may try rewarding our kids for "good" behavior in hopes that this will convince them to stop acting out in the future.

Yet, although these responses might "work" in the short term by bringing about desired behavior change, they function as ineffective stopgaps as they fail to help kids manage the emotions that led them to misbehave or melt down in the first place. In other words, when we try to nip behavior in the bud in this way, we leave the roots of the behavior intact and can thus expect more of it, even if in a different form or at a later time. Indeed, if we focus on eliminating undesirable behaviors without addressing the emotions driving them, then these emotions will either remain or continue to pop up and overpower our children's executive centers (and potentially ours, too) at some point in the future.

Of note, however, it's not just parents who tend to take this kind of approach to challenging behaviors. Even many expert clinical psychologists who specialize in working with families claim that the best way to deal with unwanted behaviors is either to ignore these behaviors while praising the good things that kids do, or if this proves to be ineffective, to punish kids for their misbehavior. And in some respects, they are right. After all, these tactics do sometimes result in behavioral improvements (though these effects are often temporary, at best).

By contrast, there seems to be much less interest among mental health professionals in examining what happens when we acknowledge and address the underlying causes of children's problematic behaviors rather than focus on eliminating them. The reason? Although conjecture, this may be a reflection of the fact that most adults view children's acting-out behaviors and dramatic emotional displays as intentional ploys that need to be quashed in order to ensure that kids don't grow up to be social deviants or emotional basket cases. Sure, this might be a bit extreme, but I do believe there is at least a tiny part of many of us that believes something along these lines. Alternatively, or in addition to this, it may be that we are so focused on quelling our own uncomfortable emotions that we don't even think to explore what might be leading our kids to engage in the behaviors that drive us mad. Instead, we simply do whatever it takes to extinguish these behaviors as quickly as possible so we can escape the feelings burning within us and avoid the judgmental glares we fear others might give us if we don't rein in our kids.

Controlling Ourselves, Not Our Kids

Regardless of the forces propelling this emphasis on behavior modification, moving away from controlling our children in this manner and focusing on controlling our *own* behaviors instead can be incredibly freeing and rewarding. Making this shift also reduces the likelihood of power struggles and helps facilitate a much stronger connection with our children. After all, just as we wouldn't appreciate a loved one nitpicking at *us* all day long, the same is true for our kids. Thus, rather than focus on getting our children to do X or to stop doing Y, we can use our energy to calm ourselves so we can better understand and respond to whatever it is our children are trying to tell us through their behaviors. Additionally, when we harness the power to control our own responses and relinquish command of things that weren't really ever ours to control in the first place, we increase the chances that our efforts will be met with success – even if only incrementally – which can in turn give a sizable boost to our sense of self-efficacy.

That said, given that we are the ones responsible for keeping our children safe and healthy, I realize this idea of giving up control over their behaviors might seem paradoxical at first. Of course, we still need to ensure that our kids do things like brush their teeth and go to school in the mornings. We also need to protect the people, pets, and valuables within our homes so that they don't get hurt or damaged by our children. Yet, taking responsibility for these things does not mean transferring this burden onto our children by insisting that they abide by our wishes at all times. Rather, as many gentle parenting experts have suggested, it involves stepping into the role as captain of our family's team and tactfully guiding us through whatever challenges we encounter, thus modeling for our kids how to one day do the same (Kennedy, 2022; Lansbury, 2014a, 2014b; Stiffelman, 2012).

So, what does this look like in practice? Once again, let me first give an example from my own life of how this ought *not* to look.

One of the things I struggled with the most in the first few months after my son was born was getting out of the house in the mornings with kids in tow so that I could get to work on time. No matter how much I prepared the night before or how early we all woke up, I simply could not seem to get my daughter to move in the mornings. Whether it was getting out of bed, getting dressed, brushing teeth, eating breakfast, putting on shoes, walking to the car, or getting into her car seat, my daughter wanted none of it. On some days, her resistance to these steps showed up in the form of unbridled silliness, whereas at other times, it took the form of a full-blown tantrum.

What remained consistent, however, was the unmistakable anger and frustration that exuded from within me in response to my daughter's apparent unwillingness to cooperate. I knew that my daughter was physically capable of doing each of these things, and it made absolutely no sense to me why she was so adamant about not doing them. I was befuddled and muddled through, hoping I could appeal to the budding logical side of her brain. If nothing else, I figured a good old-fashioned guilt trip might do the trick. I therefore let her know repeatedly how many people were counting on us to arrive on time each morning and how much more stressful it made my day when we were late. I also spent many of our drives together recounting each of the things that had or hadn't happened that morning that had left us rushing, proclaiming after each one the best way to troubleshoot these hiccups moving forward. Almost always, my self-generated solutions involved my daughter doing a better job "listening" to my requests.

As you can imagine, this approach did little more than strain my relationship with my daughter and fuel my frustration with her. I'm also fairly certain that it left my daughter feeling pretty terrible about herself, not to mention angry with me. I hated how our mornings were going and yet, for months, I remained stuck trying to get my daughter to do what she was clearly showing me she couldn't do – at least not since becoming a big sister – without additional help.

While I can't say exactly when or how I realized that it was my approach to our mornings that needed to change, I can tell you that when I finally did, our mornings became a whole lot less stressful for all of us. Rather than push back against my daughter's resistance by insisting that she "hurry up," I started focusing on calming myself enough to be able to non-judgmentally inquire as to what was going on for her so we could work together as a team to get out the door. Although these chats took precious minutes that I initially thought I didn't have to spare, they ended up saving loads of time by helping me identify and meet the underlying needs driving my daughter's resistance, thus obviating it altogether on many days. Further, on days when my anger and frustration mounted, it felt incredibly empowering to practice remaining in control of myself, rather than letting my emotions control me. Years later, it still does.

Admittedly, I'm not always able to stay as calm as I'd like in the mornings. Yet, because I still falter in this regard, I can confidently say that how I respond to my kids' morning resistance is the key determining factor for both whether we get out the door on time *and* how we feel about each other when we say goodbye for the day. And while I sometimes wish that this weren't the case – that my behavior didn't matter quite so much – accepting this reality has opened the door for me to grow in ways that I never imagined I could.

Nevertheless, I know all too well how challenging it can be to refrain from acting on our own unhelpful urges to yell, scold, or shame our kids when feeling flooded ourselves. In fact, sometimes it seems downright impossible to inhibit these urges. However, even though we all blow our lids at times, there is always a way to cool our emotions (even if only a smidge) so we don't lose it with our kids. The trick is simply to remember that we don't have to let our emotions call the shots so that we can select and utilize skills to thwart this hijacking. Although this is certainly easier said than done, especially when caring for young children, the upshot is that it *is* possible, thanks to a plethora of evidence-based strategies that were designed for this very purpose. Accordingly, in the coming chapters, you will find a host of science-backed tools for skillfully navigating the many emotional storms we face as parents.

A Word of Caution

Before delving into these strategies, it's worth discussing what self-control is and what it is *not*, given that misguided attempts in this regard can easily backfire, making life harder for both us and our kids. A common misconception about self-control is that it involves being able to turn off inconvenient emotions when they arise, especially when these feelings aren't serving us well. In fact, most of the people who see me for therapy do so because they want to *stop* feeling so anxious, angry, sad, etc. They are convinced that they shouldn't be feeling these emotions, at least not so intensely, and they are desperate for some relief. After all, we are evolutionarily programmed to avoid pain, be it physical or emotional. Thus, when unwanted emotions surface, it's natural to want to undo or put an end to whatever is triggering these feelings. Unfortunately, however, these well-intentioned attempts to reduce or avoid emotional suffering tend to amplify and maintain our distress, particularly in the long run.

To illustrate, let's start with a non-parenting example. If I'm anxious and worry that my partner doesn't love me anymore, I might try to take control of the situation and ease my anxiety by asking my partner if he still loves me. Although I might feel some momentary relief if and when he reassures me that he loves me very much, my anxiety is likely to shoot back up again the next time I have the thought that he might not love me anymore. And since asking for reassurance helped me feel less anxious in the past, I am likely to try to get my partner to give me this reassurance whenever this thought arises again. Not exactly sexy, huh? In the long term, this might lead my partner to feel annoyed with my constant questioning, potentially making it hard for him to continue loving me. If nothing else, my attempts to reduce my anxiety prevent me from learning that I can tolerate emotional distress without giving in to the unhelpful urges that tend to accompany it, thus rendering me captive to my own unwanted emotions.

Interestingly, a very similar process occurs when we try to control our children in order to reduce our own discomfort. Specifically, when we react emotionally to our children's challenging behaviors in an attempt to squash these, we dysregulate our kids even further, thus potentially leading them to act out even more. This, in turn, usually intensifies our own emotions, as well as our urges to exert even more control. It also reinforces our brain's wiring to respond in this ineffective manner and leads us to falsely conclude that we can't tolerate the uncomfortable emotions our kids sometimes trigger in us without giving in to the unhelpful urges that come with these feelings. As a result, we end up reeling and grasping for control again each time our kids act out in the future, just as I used to on the regular when trying to get out of the house with my kids in the mornings.

Thus, when I talk about self-control, I am referring to control of our behaviors – not our emotions. In other words, self-control is not about suppressing or shooing away negative emotions or the triggers for these, but rather feeling and accepting these when they arise within us while continuing to treat our children with unconditional love and respect. (Of note, a neat side effect of allowing our ideal selves – rather than whatever we're feeling in the moment – to guide our actions is that doing so can sometimes indirectly cool our own challenging emotions.)

Luckily, although willpower alone cannot rewire our brains to respond in this way when we are feeling intense emotions, lots and lots of practice acting opposite to our controlling urges can. But first, we have to believe that *we* are the ones who need to change. We also need skills to help us regulate our emotions so that we can break the unhelpful habits we've developed in our interactions with our kids.

Skills for Turning Down the Heat (and Keeping It Low)

To assist you in becoming a more emotionally savvy parent, I've packed this book with a number of science-backed tools for getting through emotional storms (ours and those of our kids), just as you might pack a bag full of gear to keep you warm and dry when venturing out in the rain. Once again, the goal is not to avoid or get rid of unwanted emotions, but rather to manage them more effectively when they arise. Thus, in the coming chapters, you will find a set of skills for accepting emotions (Chapter 3), a set of skills for regulating emotions (Chapter 4), and a set of skills for tolerating emotions (Chapter 5). In brief, these are tools for being more present and emotionally agile in our day-to-day lives so we can skillfully navigate whatever stressors we encounter, thus enabling us to live in ways that more closely align with the parents (and people) we want to be. Each set of skills serves a unique function and is comprised of a number of mini-skills that, like an umbrella, can be taken with us and used anytime, anywhere. Indeed, even if life seems breezy for you at the moment, these skills can still be tremendously helpful in deepening and extending the sense of peace and harmony that you are feeling, while also preparing you for whatever storms may be heading your way.

The skills for accepting emotions enable us to welcome whatever we (or our kids) are feeling while continuing to act in ways that are congruent with our values. Complementing this set, the skills for regulating emotions enable us to reduce our vulnerability to experiencing intense, negative emotions in the first place and allow us to modulate our own challenging emotions when they do arise and aren't serving us well. Finally, the skills for tolerating emotions enable us to sit with intense distress without giving in to our urges to explode or engage in other maladaptive coping mechanisms that usually leave us and our kids feeling worse, not better.

Although there are no hard-and-fast rules for when to use which skill or combination of skills, as a general rule of thumb, the more dysregulated we are, the more skills we will likely need. And given that some skills require more cognitive resources than others, it can be helpful in moments of dysregulation to start by using those that don't require all that much brain power to quickly dampen arousal before layering on additional skills.

For example, when my daughter pushed my son into a creek many feet below him in the infamous summer of 2020, I used a number of skills over the next few moments in order to cool the intense anger that was pulling for me to scold and shame her. First, I noticed and accepted my anger and paid attention to what it felt like in my body. Next, I slowed down my breathing and said the word "choose" on each inhalation and the word "love" on each exhalation as I pulled my son out of the creek, thus helping me tolerate my anger while resisting the urge to unleash it on my daughter. Lastly, I regulated my anger by reminding myself that my daughter clearly needed some help. This, in turn, enabled me to make a conscious choice to act lovingly toward her and communicate through my body language, words, and tone of voice that I was on her side and there to keep everyone safe.

Of course, we won't always be able to accept, regulate, and tolerate the emotions rising in our household. On some days, the pull from our own emotions will be so great that we will resort to using whatever quick fixes we can think of to get our children to stop doing the things that are dysregulating us. How do I know? Because I – the expert in emotion regulation who is trying to convince you to give up trying to change your kids – still revert to using these tactics myself at times, despite the fact that they almost always end up making my day significantly harder. Fortunately, however, perfection is not the goal here, nor is it realistic.

That said, the more we can prioritize and practice accepting, regulating, and tolerating emotions over other agendas we might have in mind, the more likely it is that these skills will become part of our permanent repertoire. Meanwhile, each time we use these skills, we find ourselves one step closer to the consistently calmer home we always dreamed we would have. Further, when we use these skills to get through the day, we not only help ourselves but we also model for our impressionable kids how to use these skills as well. Sure, it may be years before we see our kids use them (if they ever do). However, the more we model these strategies, the more likely it is that our kids will one day come to rely on them, too.

When Unhelpful Thoughts Get in the Way

Despite our best intentions to practice using the skills in this book, we all experience automatic, unhelpful thoughts at times that can fan the flames of dysregulation and make it hard for us to be our most skillful selves. These thoughts skew toward the negative and are considered universal and evolutionarily hardwired. Known as the "negativity bias," this tendency to notice and dwell on the negative allows us to readily detect and respond to any dangers we encounter, thus increasing our chances of survival (Vaish et al., 2008).

Due to its adaptive significance, this bias frequently emerges even when our survival isn't on the line (Baumeister et al., 2001). For example, we might jump to the conclusion that a friend is mad at us because they didn't say "hi" when we passed them on the street, without even considering the possibility that they simply didn't see us. As a result, we can experience negative thoughts or interpretations about anything or anyone, including our children, sometimes even without our awareness. This means that even the most adoring parents will have unfavorable thoughts about their kids from time to time.

Although the presence of negative thoughts about our kids isn't necessarily problematic in and of itself, these unhelpful thoughts warrant discussion as they can hinder our ability to use the skills discussed here if left unchecked. For instance, if I believe my daughter is being mean when she teases her brother, then I might find myself feeling so angry with her that I wind up scolding her. On the other hand, if I see my daughter's teasing as a sign that she must be having a tough time, then I am much more likely to be able to take a more skillful, loving, and helpful approach. In other words, the automatic, negative thoughts that we all sometimes have about our children can adversely impact not only how we feel about our kids but also how we act toward them.

Indeed, it turns out that our thoughts, feelings, and behaviors are all interconnected (Beck, 2021; Gillihan, 2018), as depicted in what is sometimes called the Cognitive Triangle (see Figure 2.1). As can be seen in this figure, the Cognitive Triangle is made up of three points – our thoughts, feelings, and behaviors – each of which influences and is influenced by the other two.

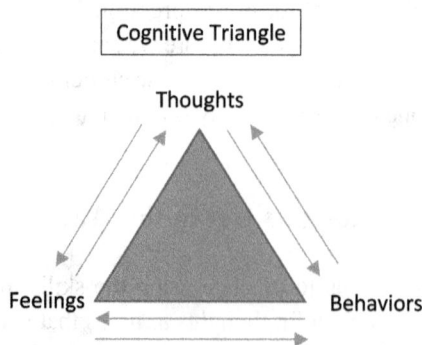

Figure 2.1 The relationships among our thoughts, feelings, and behaviors.

Cognitive Triangle

I think: I'm sick of this!

I feel
angry

I yell at
my son

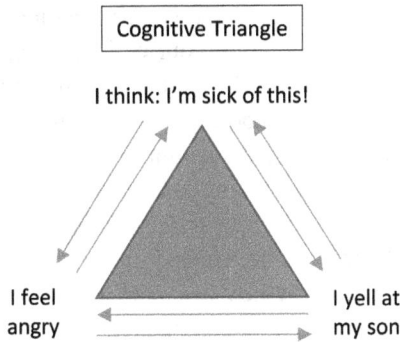

Figure 2.2 Cognitive Triangle with the thought "I'm sick of this!"

With the caveat that it is not always possible to tell which of these components occurs first (and that our emotions and behaviors can just as easily serve as the impetus for our thoughts), let's take a closer look at the role that our negative thoughts sometimes have in catalyzing this process.

Like many kids, when my son was a toddler, he would sometimes throw his toys when he was upset. So, let's imagine that my son is throwing toys, and I think to myself that I am sick of him doing things he knows he shouldn't do. Even if this thought remains subconscious (i.e., out of my awareness), it might lead me to become angry with my son and yell at him (see Figure 2.2), thus adding a heap of anger, sadness, and shame to the already overwhelming cocktail of emotions that likely led him to throw his toys in the first place.

Further, instead of connecting with him and trying to understand what's going on from his perspective, I end up placing a wedge between us, thereby missing a valuable opportunity to help him process and release his feelings in a more constructive manner. Moreover, if he continues throwing toys and I angrily scold him and carry him to the corner for a time-out, then I inadvertently model for him that it's okay to "lose it" when feeling upset with others, while also unintentionally conveying to him that my love is conditional and contingent upon him pleasing me. Additionally, by giving in to my anger and letting it control my behavior in this manner, I end up feeding it, thus enabling it to grow and stick around for longer than I'd like. This, in turn, makes my job harder and significantly less enjoyable, while also fueling more negative thoughts about my son.

How do I know? Because, over the years I have had plenty of negative thoughts about my kids and have repeatedly fallen into the trap of believing that *their* behaviors needed to change, not mine. Unfortunately, every time I have let these thoughts creep in I have prolonged my misery (as well as my children's) and have thrown what feels like a wrench into my relationship with them. And given that you are reading this book, my guess is that you have also tried targeting your children's challenging behaviors with limited success and that this has left you with a number of unpleasant, negative thoughts and feelings about your kids – and maybe even yourself.

Again, however, just because it's natural and common for us to find fault with our kids does not mean that doing so is helpful. After all, as the Cognitive Triangle suggests, when we criticize our kids – either out loud or in our heads – for the things they do or don't do, we end up feeling more negatively about them, which can lead us to treat them in a more negative manner. Additionally, having our children at the center of a negative cycle like this can, for many of us, give rise to a similar cycle revolving around ourselves (and vice versa).

An Empowering Reframe

So, does this mean we should tell ourselves that it's no big deal if our kids throw toys when this could result in them breaking things or hurting others? Or, more generally, that we should let our kids walk all over us and do whatever they want? Absolutely not! Instead, what I am suggesting is taking the time to calmly and non-judgmentally explore the causes of our children's behaviors before trying to modify them. After all, behavior is a form of communication. If we don't understand what our kids are trying to communicate, we are unlikely to make any real dent in their behaviors, now or in the future, as we won't be able to help our children meet the needs that are driving these behaviors.

Although this reframe might not sink in immediately, the cognitive-behavioral strategies you'll find in this book can be extremely helpful in facilitating this pivot. Returning to the Cognitive Triangle, if we can change just one of the points in the figure, then we can bring about change in the others. Fortunately, even though we might not be able to directly turn off our anger when our kids act out, we can shift the lens through which we view our children and their behavior, which, in turn, can enable us to adopt a more accepting, curious, and calm way of responding to them.

For instance, we can train our brains to think about our kids' behaviors in the same way that we might view the actions (or lack thereof) of a friend who is going through a divorce or a sibling who is battling cancer. Just as we would give friends and loved ones facing hardship the benefit of the doubt and trust that they will do better or more if and when they are able to do so, we can be more forgiving with our kids as well. Specifically, we can give our children permission to fall apart when feeling overwhelmed and trust that they will do better if and when they are emotionally and developmentally ready to do so.

Of course, flipping the story that we tell ourselves about our children and their behaviors is not something we can do in one fell swoop. Indeed, changing our mindset in this way requires lots of time and practice. Plus, even when we do finally manage to shift our perspective, this change is unlikely to be permanent. Whether due to the presence of intense emotional arousal or the return of the negativity bias, we can expect unhelpful, negative thoughts about our children to pop up again and again. Thankfully, however, the more we practice reframing these thoughts when they surface, the easier it becomes to do so.

With this in mind, let's turn back to the example of my son throwing toys. Rather than focus on how fed up I am with this behavior or on how unacceptable it is, I can tell myself that my guy must be struggling in some way and that he needs my help. Maybe he's frustrated or angry and doesn't yet know how to express or manage these feelings in a more skillful way. Or maybe his toy throwing is serving to communicate something else entirely. Either way, I can remind myself that his developing executive center clearly isn't yet able to reliably inhibit his urge to throw toys (at least not under the current circumstances) and can step in to help him with this. For instance, I can calmly move closer to him and gently block him from picking up or throwing any additional toys, while empathically letting him know that I can tell he is angry and that I am there to help keep him and others, including me, safe (see Figure 2.3). I might offer for him to throw a soft ball instead of a hard toy or I might just sit with him while he cries, throws himself on the floor, yells, or tells me all of the reasons why he is so upset. And I can give him as much space and time as he needs, knowing that no emotion can last forever and that his anger will eventually subside once he has had a chance to fully release it.

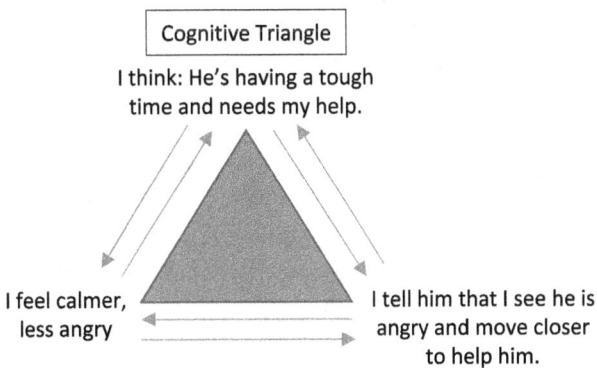

Cognitive Triangle

I think: He's having a tough
time and needs my help.

I feel calmer,
less angry

I tell him that I see he is
angry and move closer
to help him.

Figure 2.3 Cognitive Triangle with the thought "He's having a tough time and needs my help."

Having sat with both of my children in this way many times, I realize what I am suggesting takes a great deal of effort and energy to put into practice. It also requires a willingness to wade into the discomfort that often arises within us when our kids are testing limits and in distress. Accordingly, I know how tempting it can be to look for a quicker fix. Yet, even if I were to find just the right tactic to get my son to stop throwing toys forever, this solution would be nothing more than a temporary bandage for my own distress. The reason? Like all of us, my son will continue to experience strong emotions, make mistakes, and do things he knows he shouldn't do for the rest of his life.

Thus, even though these moments aren't easy, they are ones I wouldn't ever want to miss as they serve as the backbone for the lifelong relationship I am trying to cultivate with my kids. When I am able to see beneath my son's toy throwing, for example, I communicate to him that I love him exactly as he is, in spite of his messy emotions and behaviors. I also teach him that his worth is not defined by his mistakes and that I can be a source of love and support even when he's messed up in some way, whether that be today or in five, ten, or twenty years. Moreover, by providing him with a safe space to feel and release his feelings, I impart to him that he can tolerate intense emotions without giving in to their accompanying urges while also helping him learn that even the biggest, most painful feelings eventually pass. Perhaps equally important, these moments serve as golden opportunities for me to practice accepting, regulating, and tolerating my own unpleasant emotions, thus strengthening my muscles for responding to distress in this new, more adaptive manner.

Again, I want to stress that it's okay if the understanding and nonjudgmental stance described here does not come naturally to you at first. After all, most of us have spent our whole lives steeped in the societal belief that the punishment must fit the crime, and thus it's unsurprising that we might grapple with this new way of viewing our children's behaviors. Further, whether we are trying to restructure unhelpful thoughts about our kids, ourselves, or the world in general, the process of modifying these thoughts almost always involves considerable time and practice. Thus, although I encourage you to try to start thinking of your children's challenging behaviors as cries for help, please know that it will likely be a while before this new way of thinking becomes your automatic, default mode.

The Responsibility Is Ours

Encouragingly, when we are able to take on this new mindset (even if only momentarily), we find ourselves better positioned to treat our kids in a way that reflects the immense love that we feel for them. This is critical as I believe that the secret to raising well-adjusted kids lies in how we treat them and what we model for them, not in the messages we stuff down their throats or in the battles we "win." Moreover, the kinder we are to our kids, the better we feel about ourselves.

It is for these reasons that I strive to treat my kids with unconditional love and respect in every interaction I have with them. This is what I aim for even when I find my kids drawing on the coffee table with permanent markers or when one of them is trying to hit, kick, bite, or tease the other. In fact, I expect to see these limit-testing behaviors, and I view them as my children's developmentally appropriate attempts to let me know they have lost their footing and need help regaining their balance. Indeed, as discussed earlier, this kind of button-pushing behavior is usually the result of a strong emotion hijacking the immature command center of their brains and pulling for actions they know are not acceptable. Consequently, yelling or administering a punishment in these moments is only going to intensify the emotion that is already flooding them, thus amplifying their state of dysregulation, as well as mine.

As a result, rather than put the onus on our kids to refrain from engaging in impulsive behaviors that their brains are not yet equipped to inhibit 100 percent of the time, it's our responsibility to try to prevent these behaviors from happening in the first place and to calmly block them from continuing when our preventive efforts fail. That is, it's on us to store our permanent markers out of our young kids' reach, just as it's on us to maintain our composure while gently prying our toddler's hands from his sister's hair when curiosity or anger compel him to try to yank it off of her scalp. Similarly, instead of testing our kids when they are clearly dysregulated by demanding that they turn off the water that they are spraying or by commanding that they stop pulling leaves off our favorite plant, it's on us to get in there and lovingly turn off the water or relocate the plant.

As is obvious from the stories shared thus far, however, I'm not always able to remain this cool, calm, and collected. When I get emotionally hijacked, it's often because my automatic, negative thoughts become too loud for me to drown out or restructure. At other times, my anger flares before I even notice what I am thinking. Yet, despite these differing causes for my own meltdowns, the common thread in these instances where I lose my cool is the glaring need for additional skills. Thankfully, there are more than enough tools to help simmer down even the hottest of tempers. We just need to learn and practice these skills enough so that using them will one day become our default response when emotional temperatures begin to climb. Thus, in the coming chapters, you will find a number of science-backed tools for navigating the emotional waves of parenting, including critical arousal-dampening strategies (a mouthful, I know) for moments when reframing thoughts simply isn't enough or even relevant.

Theoretical Roots

Before continuing, I want to acknowledge that my approach to parenting is not something I dreamed up entirely on my own, but is instead a synthesis of key theories and findings from the fields of clinical and developmental psychology fused with ideas from a type of gentle parenting known as "respectful parenting" (Lansbury, 2014a, 2014b). Respectful parenting – which has been written about most extensively by parenting expert Janet Lansbury – differs dramatically from the traditional styles of parenting most of us know from our own childhoods. Unlike more conventional parenting approaches, in which the goal is often to get kids to do what we as parents want, respectful parenting prioritizes developing an authentic, collaborative relationship with our children that is based on acceptance and trust. In a nutshell, it encourages parents to create a nurturing environment that allows children to develop at their own pace and in their own unique ways. To this end, it involves observing kids with curiosity – rather than trying to direct or control their every move – and welcoming every one of their emotions, no matter how excessive, messy, dark, or inconvenient these feelings might seem. It also involves calmly setting and holding firm limits when needed, while refraining from using rewards, excessive praise, distraction, bribes, threats, punishments, and other mainstream control tactics.

Although respectful parenting has not been tested scientifically to date, it aligns closely with the empirically supported parenting technique known as "emotion coaching" (Gottman, 1997), which encourages parents to view children's intense emotional displays as opportunities for teaching and connection. Like respectful parenting, emotion coaching involves noticing, acknowledging, and validating children's feelings while setting limits and helping children problem-solve how to manage their emotions and navigate triggering situations. Notably, children whose parents use emotion coaching are better at regulating their emotions, have fewer behavioral problems, are higher academic achievers, and are more socially competent than children of non-emotion coaching parents (Gottman et al., 1996; Shortt et al., 2010). Additionally, training parents in emotion coaching results in improvements in parents' and children's emotion regulation abilities, as well as reductions in children's behavioral problems (Wilson et al., 2012).

As this data suggests, better developmental trajectories unfold for both kids and parents when we are able to non-judgmentally accept and welcome our children's emotions while holding appropriate limits. It is important to note, however, that emotion coaching is a technique for responding to children's emotions, specifically; it is not as comprehensive of an approach as respectful parenting. As a result, emotion coaching leaves it up to us, as parents, to figure out how to move through moments in the day when our children aren't particularly charged but we are.

For example, emotion coaching isn't all that useful when *we* are stressed and rushing to get out of the house to start our day but our kids just want to stay at home and play . . . all . . . day . . . long. Similarly, emotion coaching offers little guidance regarding how to interact with our kids during routine moments when emotions aren't particularly intense, such as when bathing, dressing, feeding, or playing with our kids. Yet, given that these moments also influence the bonds we form, it would be helpful to have a science-backed guide for navigating all of the various interactions we have with our children. Thankfully, respectful parenting not only aligns with emotion coaching but also fills in some of the holes not covered by it.

Further, respectful parenting's mindful, all-feelings-allowed stance also converges beautifully with the science-backed practices that I utilize in my work as a clinical psychologist. That said, although respectful parenting certainly gives us a leg up in managing the emotional waves of parenting, many parents who try to adopt this approach still struggle to manage their emotions when with their kids. Thus, this book not only aligns with key tenets from respectful parenting, but also presents state-of-the-art emotion regulation skills from the field of clinical psychology that will give you the tools you need to become a more emotionally agile, respectful parent. In fact, as noted in the Introduction, I conceptualize Emotion-Savvy Parenting as a natural extension of the evidence-based, cognitive-behavioral treatments that I provide in my clinical practice more than anything else.

From Roots to Fruits

Perhaps more important than the origins of Emotion-Savvy Parenting is where it can get you. Although we have no way of knowing exactly what the future will hold for you or your family should you embrace this approach, we do have a large body of research suggesting that the theories and skills that comprise it can help you become a more emotionally agile individual. And as with anything, the more you practice implementing what you read here, the more the benefits are likely to accrue. Will the work be easy? Almost certainly not. As we've already established, parenting is hard no matter how you go about it. My wish for you, however, is that Emotion-Savvy Parenting will enable you to better enjoy the fruits of your labor and bring about a greater sense of fulfillment to your life as a parent. If nothing else, may you and your children find the freedom that comes with knowing you don't have to be governed by the emotions that visit your home. And now with that said, on to the skills!

References

Baumeister, R. F., Bratslavsky, E., Finkenauer, C., & Vohs, K. D. (2001). Bad is stronger than good. *Review of General Psychology, 5*(4), 323–370. https://doi.org/10.1037/1089-2680.5.4.323

Beck, J. S. (2021). *Cognitive behavior therapy: Basics and beyond* (3rd ed.). The Guilford Press.

Casey, B. J., Jones, R. M., & Hare, T. A. (2008). The adolescent brain. *Annals of the New York Academy of Sciences, 1124*, 111–126. https://doi.org/10.1196/annals.1440.010

Gillihan, S. J. (2018). *Cognitive behavioral therapy made simple: 10 strategies for managing anxiety, depression, anger, panic and worry*. Althea Press.

Gottman, J. M. (1997). *Raising an emotionally intelligent child*. Simon & Schuster Paperbacks.

Gottman, J. M., Katz, L. F., & Hooven, C. (1996). Parental meta-emotion philosophy and the emotional life of families: Theoretical models and preliminary data. *Journal of Family Psychology, 10*, 243–268. https://doi.org/10.1037/0893-3200.10.3.243

Greene, R. (2016). *Raising human beings: Creating a collaborative partnership with your child*. Scribner.

Greene, R. (2021). *The explosive child: A new approach for understanding and parenting easily frustrated, chronically inflexible children* (6th ed.). Harper Collins.

Kennedy, B. (2022). *Good inside: A guide to becoming the parent you want to be*. Harper Thorsons.

Lansbury, J. (2014a). *Elevating child care: A guide to respectful parenting*. CreateSpace Publishing.

Lansbury, J. (2014b). *No bad kids: Toddler discipline without shame*. CreateSpace Publishing.

Shortt, J. W., Stoolmiller, M., Smith-Shine, J. N., Mark Eddy, J., & Sheeber, L. (2010). Maternal emotion coaching, adolescent anger regulation, and siblings' externalizing symptoms. *Journal of Child Psychology and Psychiatry*, *51*, 799–808. https://doi.org/10.1111/j.1469-7610.2009.02207.x

Stiffelman, S. (2012). *Parenting without power struggles: Raising joyful, resilient kids while staying calm, cool, and connected*. Atria Books.

Vaish, A., Grossman, T., & Woodward, A. (2008). Not all emotions are created equal: The negativity bias in social-emotional development. *Psychological Bulletin*, *134*(3), 383–403. https://doi.org/10.1037/0033-2909.134.3.383

Wilson, K. R., Havighurst, S. S., & Harley, A. E. (2012). Tuning into kids: An effectiveness trial of a parenting program targeting emotion socialization of preschoolers. *Journal of Family Psychology*, *26*, 56–65. https://doi.org/10.1037/a0026480

Part 2

The ART (Accept, Regulate, Tolerate) and Science of Emotions

Acceptance

3

The Catalyst of Change

Alice, a busy executive and a mom of three young, rambunctious boys, came to see me years ago due to feeling anxious and overwhelmed with life. Although her anxiety was the primary focus of our therapy, she shared in our first meeting her disappointment with how life as a mom was shaking out for her. Like so many other parents, when Alice was expecting her first son, she imagined herself having a blissfully fun and loving relationship with him and with the other kids she hoped to one day have as well. And of course, she dreamed her kids would be sweet, playful, and easygoing children who would get along beautifully with each other at just about all times. Sure, she knew there would be hard moments here and there, but these rarely made it into the highlight reel of Sunday morning snuggles, bathtime giggles, and exciting games of tag that played in her mind whenever she pictured her future life as a mom.

Alas, nine years into motherhood, Alice confided that she felt dismayed by how stark the contrast was between what she had envisioned and her actual experience as a parent. With tears in her eyes, she confessed that she felt disheartened and frustrated that her boys were not, at all times, the happy, compliant, and enthralling beings she assumed they would be. Instead, they often seemed intractably silly or unreasonably angry, and they sometimes did things she was certain they knew they shouldn't be doing, leaving her concerned that they weren't developing as they should be. Likewise, she worried there must be something wrong with her because she wasn't enjoying every waking hour with her "precious bundles." In

DOI: 10.4324/9781003428343-6

truth, although she relished occasional moments with her kids, she frequently dreaded her time with them and spent much of it feeling bored, impatient, or irritable, as well as guilty for having these feelings she believed no good mom should feel.

As is the case for many parents, Alice wanted only the best for her boys and worked hard trying to please all three of them, only to find that she could rarely make even just one happy. Her house seemed to be filled with constant bickering, and even the most special, well-planned outings usually devolved into full-on kid brawls. Yet, although her boys appeared to make each other miserable the majority of the time, they resisted any attempts at separation and almost always wound up back together when instructed to spend time apart, as though some magnetic force existed between them. When she tried to have one-on-one time with one of them, the other two would complain – verbally or through their actions – that it wasn't fair. *They* wanted time with her! Once, her six-year-old even kicked a hole in the living room wall because he was so upset that Alice was helping his older brother with homework instead of playing with him.

This and other similarly destructive incidents left Alice feeling as though she couldn't take a second to herself without risking her entire house burning down. She felt obligated to ensure that all three boys were thoroughly occupied at all times, and she found herself feeling increasingly burnt out from playing the demanding and often incongruous roles of entertainer and referee. Her fuse appeared to be growing shorter and shorter with each passing day, and she could not seem to break the habit of nitpicking and yelling at her kids, which she had begun doing much more than she cared to admit. She felt ashamed and defeated, and though she loved her boys immensely, she sometimes secretly wished she hadn't had them in the first place.

The Harsh Reality

Alice's sense of disillusionment is one to which most parents can relate. The discordance between our imagined and actual lives as parents makes it difficult for us to accept not only our kids but also the uncomfortable feelings that they sometimes stir up within us. Unfortunately, however, pushing for things to be the way we think they should be rarely serves us well. In fact, when troubled by the circumstances we face as parents, the wisest, most effective response is usually to accept things exactly as they are. Interestingly, adopting this accepting stance can, on its own, lighten the emotional load we carry as parents and help us deepen the connections we have with our kids. Having said that, if you're noticing a big reaction to these last few sentences, please know you're not alone in that reaction and hang tight for more on this!

Acceptance Defined

Although the word "acceptance" can be defined in many different ways, when used by psychologists, it is typically defined as acknowledging reality or what is factually true without judgment (Linehan, 2015). Critically, this definition of acceptance has nothing to do with approving, liking, or agreeing with one's circumstances, but simply involves recognizing the facts as they are. You don't have to be excited or happy about these facts; you just need to acknowledge them without trying to ignore, reject, evaluate, or change them.

For instance, you can accept that a loved one has died while very much wishing they were still here. Or you might accept that you can't have the picnic you planned in the park given that a thunderstorm is raging outside, even though you were hoping the weather wouldn't interfere with your plans. Similarly, as parents, we can accept our kids' meltdowns and tantrums, no matter how unpleasant or inconvenient we may find them, just as we can accept our kids' tears at morning daycare drop-off while hoping that the transition will get easier with time.

What to Accept

Keeping this definition in mind, let's move on to discussing what sorts of things I recommend aiming to accept. First and foremost, while I'd never advocate for accepting violent or destructive behavior, we can always accept the feelings underlying these behaviors, as well as every other feeling that shows up for us and others. We can also strive to accept our thoughts, as well as others' thoughts, even if we disagree with these or don't believe them to be true. Although there are many reasons for this, perhaps the biggest one is that trying to reject or argue away a thought that we or others believe rarely works.

For example, if your daughter says she's scared that there's a monster under her bed and you respond by saying there's no need to worry because monsters don't exist, she's likely going to find herself wondering a short while later how you can be so sure. After all, what if you are wrong? Or, if your son believes he's stupid because he failed his math test and you tell him he's the smartest kid you know, he very well may laugh or slam the door in your face, but he's certainly not going to conclude that you are right.

Furthermore, when we push against our kids' thoughts, we run the risk of inadvertently invalidating their experience and sending the message that we don't believe what they tell us. For instance, if my son says he hates his sister and I respond by saying, "No, you don't!" there's a good chance that he's going to dig in his heels and insist – perhaps more intensely this time – that he really does hate her. And the truth is, in moments of anger, he might really believe he hates his sister. However, if I continue arguing otherwise, he's likely going to become even more dysregulated, which may, in turn, make it hard for me to regulate my own emotions.

Thus, rather than try to debunk these kinds of expressions, we're much better off accepting our kids' strong words as manifestations of the feelings underlying them. In other words, I can accept that my son is so angry with his sister right now that he *thinks* he hates her, even though I know that they'll likely be back to being best friends in no time. And I can convey this acceptance with a short and sweet statement that acknowledges his feelings such as, "You're really mad at your sister!" without trying to change his experience. Although not the goal here, this validation of our children's feelings as understandable (even if we would feel differently) can go a long way toward decreasing their distress, thus making it easier for us to stay calm.

In addition to accepting thoughts and feelings, it can also be incredibly freeing to accept behaviors that fall outside of our control, including others' words and the volume with which they speak them. This does not mean that you can never politely ask your kids to use indoor voices or point out to your son that his sister looks sad when he says he wants to chop her up into a million pieces. It also doesn't mean that you have to let your toddler screech at the top of her lungs throughout a theatrical performance or while out to dinner. However, unless we resort to sticking duct tape over our kids' mouths and handcuffing their hands so they can't rip it off, we have no way of preventing our kids from saying, singing, or shouting whatever words, noises, or songs they choose. In other words, though we may not always like what comes out of our kids' mouths, they have the ability – and I would argue the right – to vocalize whatever and however they wish, even if we may sometimes need to remove our kids from a given situation (such as a theater or a fancy restaurant) so they don't disturb others. More on this to come.

First, however, I want to circle back to other behaviors that fall outside of our control, including those involving decisions that aren't ours to make, such as how much our kids eat from their dinner plates, and as they get older, whether they choose to wear clothes that match or not, and which (if any) extracurricular activities or teams they join. Of course, this is far from a comprehensive list of choices that our kids get (and should be able) to make without judgment from us, even if different from what we might choose for ourselves. In fact, I'd argue that the longer the list of behaviors we strive to accept from our kids, the better – provided these behaviors aren't harming anyone or anything.

That said, although we can't fully dictate what our kids do or don't do in any given moment, we can (and should) block, prevent, and/or stop potentially disruptive, dangerous, or damaging actions when possible, all while accepting the feelings and impulses driving these behaviors. For example, you can calmly place yourself between your child and a peer on the playground when your child seems intent on grabbing the ball that's in the other child's hand. And you can do so while accepting the frustration your child feels about not being able to have the ball. You might say, "You really want that ball! I see that. I can't let you grab it from that boy, and you're upset that you can't play with it right now. I totally get it." Likewise, when you find your tween hitting his little sister because she drew rainbows and hearts all over his homework, you can insert yourself between your kids and block any additional hits that come while calmly saying, "Whoa, I'm not going to let you hit your sister, and I'm sorry I wasn't there to stop her from drawing on your homework. I'd be upset, too, if someone else doodled all over my work." Again, the point here is that we can accept and validate our kids' feelings and impulses (without judgment), even if we can't always permit them to act on these internal experiences.

Why Bother?

I know, I know, sometimes our kids do things that we just can't help but judge. They whine incessantly because you won't let them have a third scoop of ice cream; they lay on the floor in the middle of the supermarket claiming that they are too tired to move even an inch more; they intentionally destroy the giant Lego project that their sibling was just moments away from completing; or they shove a younger kid on the playground for "moving too slowly" through the equipment. Let's be honest, it's hard to not judge our kids at times like these. After all, we're human . . . just like them.

Having said that, imagine being the kid on the receiving end of these judgments. You've just finished your bowl of ice cream and you only want one tiny scoop more, but when you ask for this, your parent snaps at you: "Stop complaining and try being grateful for a change!" Or you're tired from multiple late nights in a row, a birthday party at a trampoline park, and a little league baseball game that your team lost, and now your mom is insisting that you spend an hour shopping with her at the grocery store after dinner, even though you can barely keep your eyes open a second longer. You collapse on the floor in the middle of the cleaning aisle while waiting for your mom to sort through a giant pile of coupons, and she starts whisper-shouting at you: "Get up now!" and then proceeds to scold you under her breath for blocking the aisle and acting like a toddler. Or, after calling you a "baby" for the umpteenth time and refusing to let you play with even one of her toys, your anger boils to the surface and you seek revenge, knocking over the Lego project your sister has been working on all day. Your parents hear the crash and come charging into the room, pulling out the harshest of tones as they reprimand you for being "naughty" and "not nice." Or you're desperate to get to the top of the jungle gym to join your friends and the toddler who isn't even old enough to be on it is blocking the only way up. You give a little shove to get him out of the way, and then your dad starts shouting in the voice that terrifies you: "What were you thinking back there? You can't shove another kid like that! Come down here right now and apologize!"

Again, take a moment to close your eyes and imagine being the kid on the receiving end of these reactions. How would your parents' responses make you feel about yourself, your parents, and your relationship with them? What emotions come up for you as you imagine yourself in these kids' shoes? Shame? Anger? Fear? Injustice? Confusion? Now imagine feeling these emotions on top of those you were likely feeling before you did the thing that gave way to such a strong reaction from your parents in the first place. What urges accompany this tangle of emotions? Do you feel like crying on the floor? Hiding? Running away? Retaliating?

If you are anything like me, your answer is likely "all of the above." This is because when others judge us negatively, we usually feel pretty lousy – not just about ourselves, but also about the person who is judging us. Although it may be hard to pinpoint each of the uncomfortable emotions that these judgments stir up in us, they certainly don't leave us feeling good or closer to the person judging us. If anything, these judgments make us want to rebel against this person, perhaps leading us to continue doing things that are likely to give rise to even more negative judgments leveled against us. Alternatively, we may feel scared of losing the other person's love and may work hard to win back their approval by hiding the parts of ourselves that they've rejected, thus inadvertently deepening the sense of disconnection that we're wanting so desperately to avoid, even though it might seem otherwise from the outside.

With this in mind, take a moment to shift gears and imagine that you are the parent in each of the aforementioned situations, judging your little one and making these judgments known to your child and all those around you. How do you feel about yourself, your child, and your relationship with your child? What emotions come up for you as you imagine yourself reacting like the parents in these examples? Shame? Anger? Fear? Injustice? Confusion? And what do these emotions leave you feeling like doing? Do you feel like crying on the floor? Hiding? Running away? Retaliating? Or are you noticing something else entirely? Maybe this book is changing how you view your own behaviors, and you are experiencing a different and unfamiliar flurry of emotions in response to this exercise.

Whatever's showing up for you, I want to stress again that we're all human and as such we're bound to judge our kids from time to time. However, as this exercise illustrates, when we do, we tend to kick up a host of painful, unwanted emotions in both us and our kids while chipping away at our connections with them. Clearly, this is far from what any of us wants.

What's more, as much as we might wish that our kids would wake up in the morning with fully developed executive centers, the reality is that our kids' brains will be developing for years and years to come (Casey et al., 2008). As a result, we can expect that they will continue to do things again and again that might easily compel us to judge them negatively if we don't strive to take a more accepting approach. After all, an immature brain is going to give way to some very immature behaviors. Thus, if we want to dial back on the emotional pain and distance that we create when we judge our kids, demanding that they stop doing the things that irk us isn't the answer. Instead, we must aim for acceptance.

Circling back to the earlier examples, if your daughter asks for another scoop of ice cream after eating the large bowl you gave her just moments ago, you can accept her desire for more by simply saying something along the lines of, "I know you really want more ice cream, and we're all done with it for tonight." Or if your son collapses on the floor in the middle of aisle five, you can accept that he's beyond exhausted and calmly offer a hand to help him up while letting him know that you'll head home soon. And if you walk into the living room and see that your son has just knocked over his sister's Lego project, you can get curious and ask him what was going on that led him to destroy her work. Lastly, if you see your daughter shove a toddler on the jungle gym, you can empathize with her, letting her know that it can be frustrating when other people are in our way, while lovingly reminding her that pushing others isn't safe.

Obviously, acceptance comes in many forms and these are just some examples of ways you might respond in these and other similar situations. That said, an approach rooted in acceptance almost always feels better than a judgmental one. Further, accepting our children's emotions also makes it easier for our kids to (eventually) accept whatever limit we've set. Accordingly, I invite you to take a moment to consider how it might feel – both for you and your kid – if you were to respond in a more accepting manner in moments like these.

The Catalyst of Change

An added benefit of acceptance is that, contrary to what many of us assume, it is actually the catalyst of change. Although this may sound paradoxical at first, think about it for a moment. In order to bring about change, we must first accept the circumstances that we'd like to be different. For instance, shortly after signing a contract to write the very book that you are currently reading, I became swamped both at work and at home. Even though I knew that I needed to be writing on a regular basis in order to meet the deadline I had agreed to in my book contract, I found myself barely writing, if at all. I made excuse after excuse for why I wasn't writing and convinced myself that the book would get done somehow, even if I didn't know how or when. However, at some point, I had to accept the inconvenient truth that my book clearly wasn't going to get done unless I started – and then continued – writing. Accepting this reality helped motivate me to take action and get writing.

Even if this exact example doesn't resonate, my guess is that you can think of other instances where you first needed to accept a problem before you could find and implement a solution to solve it. Maybe you had a physical injury and had to come to terms with the painful fact that it wasn't getting better on its own before committing to going to the doctor and doing physical therapy as prescribed. Or perhaps you needed to admit to yourself that your ten-year-old car really was making a weird sound (and that the noise you had been hearing for weeks wasn't just in your head) before finally taking it into the shop for the expensive and inconvenient repair that it clearly required. Or given that you are reading this book, it may be that after trying one traditional parenting technique after another, you reached the disappointing conclusion that these practices don't work for you, your kids, or your family and decided to seek out alternative approaches such as the one described here. Whatever the circumstances, chances are you can think of at least one instance where acceptance of some undesirable fact proved to be the very ingredient needed in order to bring about the change you desired.

Taking this a step further, acceptance not only enables us to change course, but it's also what helps us get back on track when we've veered off the path we've decided to follow. As I've said before, no matter which parenting philosophy you subscribe to, you are going to make mistakes as a parent. We all will. However, if we make excuses for these mistakes or try to forget about them, we'll likely make the same mistakes again and again. Indeed, we must first acknowledge and accept our missteps if we want to try to correct them. And while I encourage acknowledging these mistakes aloud in the presence of your children and repairing any damage done (as I discuss in Chapter 8), at the very least, it's important to privately own up to these if you hope to do better in the future. That said, regardless of how you choose to navigate these moments, the key is to do so without berating or judging yourself for the missteps you make. Again, on the off chance that this hasn't sunk in yet, we are all human and are thus bound to make mistakes as parents. Loads of them.

Returning to Acceptance

Of course, acceptance is not a one-and-done sort of thing. In other words, you may find yourself accepting something one minute and then saying it shouldn't have happened moments later. Learning to recognize (or accept) when you've moved away from acceptance, however, is usually the first step toward accepting more. For instance, years ago I had a nasty fall while walking on an icy path and practically flipped in the air, landing right on my back. Since then, I have struggled off and on with back pain, which I believe is likely, at least in part, the result of that very fall. Although I am usually able to accept this pain and the fact that the fall happened in the first place, sometimes I find myself trying to think of ways I could have prevented the fall, as though I'm trying to undo it altogether. I've even gone so far as to decide that my back pain is a thing of the past – when that's definitely not the case – in order to give myself permission to do things I once loved, only to find myself riddled with pain shortly thereafter. This return of pain, though frustrating and quite debilitating at times, usually reminds me to come back to accepting the fact that I do, indeed, have back problems and that I need to be careful in choosing activities so that I don't make things worse.

Similarly, although Alice discovered a new sense of freedom when we began discussing acceptance in our sessions, she found it hard at times to remember to bring this lens with her in her day-to-day interactions with her kids. For Alice – and just about every parent I've ever had the pleasure of working with – acceptance tends to come and go, especially at first. When calm and well-rested, Alice found it relatively easy and natural to accept her kids and their feelings, as well as her own. However, when stressed, hungry, sleep deprived, or rushed, Alice struggled to accept her kids' fighting and "not listening." Further, the more egregious, unreasonable, embarrassing, or potentially dangerous her kids' behaviors, the more difficult she found it to remember to accept the *feelings* underlying them.

This makes sense as it's easier to accept things that don't impact us all that much. For instance, if you were to lose a penny, you likely wouldn't think much of it before moving on with your day. By contrast, if you were to lose a $100 bill, you would probably be at least a little (if not very) upset and have a harder time getting past this. After all, you could use that bill for so many essential (and non-essential) purchases, making its loss harder to digest than that of the fairly useless penny. Likewise, when it comes to parenting, the more that we or others feel the sting of that which we are trying to accept, the more challenging the pill of acceptance becomes to swallow. Thankfully, we can become more accepting of just about anything – no matter how difficult or unpleasant – by returning to acceptance each time we find ourselves fighting or rejecting reality.

Mindful Acceptance

Moving away from parenting for a moment, let's talk about mindfulness (Eeles & Walker, 2022; Linehan, 2015), which is a skill that you can use to help you become more accepting in your day-to-day life – whether you are with your kids or not. Yes, I know that mindfulness is a bit of a buzzword these days, but unless you have extensive training in it, there's a good chance that you have only a vague and partially incorrect understanding of it, if that. So, before diving into how mindfulness can help you adopt a more accepting stance, let's start by defining what it actually is, as well as what it isn't.

At the most basic level, mindfulness can be defined as the act of paying attention on purpose, without judgment or attachment, to the present moment as experienced through any one or all of your five senses. In other words, it's about allowing yourself to experience reality – whether that's what's happening within or outside of you – exactly as it is without trying to control the moment and without letting judgments or thoughts about the past or the future cloud how you view it.

Further, as life experience plus a growing body of research suggests, since we can't really give our full attention to anything when multitasking, mindfulness involves intentionally focusing on one present-moment thing or activity at a time. For instance, if you decide to practice being mindful of your breath, your job is to simply pay attention to your breath – not to send an email to your boss, bake cookies, or help your toddler blow her nose. Similarly, if you choose to take a mindful walk, you'd want to aim to walk without distraction. This means that you'd walk while paying attention to what you see, hear, and/or feel and that you'd do so without scrolling on Instagram, texting your sister, or rehearsing the job talk you're giving the next day.

Now before continuing, I want to note that although multitasking is essentially the antithesis of mindfulness, contrary to what many believe, practicing mindfulness does not require going off to sit in a secluded place in silence with your eyes closed for 30 minutes or more. It is not meditation, although meditation is a form of mindfulness in which one quietly sits or stands for a period of time. Of course, if meditation is your cup of tea, by all means do it! That said, if you are anything like me, you can barely find time to shower, let alone find time to sneak away for a prolonged silent meditation. That's one of the reasons I'm such a fan of mindfulness. In contrast to meditation, which requires removing oneself from the hustle and bustle of daily life for a set amount of time, mindfulness is something that can be practiced anytime, anywhere. In fact, one of the goals of mindfulness is to help you drop into the present moment in order to enable you to more clearly see what's actually in front of you. There's no need to close your eyes or find a quiet place to practice. Instead, it's something you can use whether you are sitting still or on the go, ideally with your eyes wide open so that you can actually take in the moment – even if that moment is one in which your kids are hurling angry words at you at the top of their lungs or testing limit after limit like it's their job (which it kind of is).

Ways to Practice

With that said, let's shift now to talking about different approaches to practicing mindfulness. Essentially, there are two main ways in which you can practice: The first is to simply **notice** or observe what's going on within or outside of you, and the second is to **participate** by throwing yourself into the moment. In many ways, this is similar to what athletes do when trying to improve their game. Whether you play sports or not, indulge me briefly and think about a basketball player working on individual skills like shooting, dribbling, or passing. While practicing each of these skills, the player is likely to pay attention to how her body is moving, as well as how it feels when she moves it. For instance, she's likely to notice whether she feels tight, sluggish, fast, strong, etc. Similarly, she's likely to pay attention to her form – for example, how she's positioning her hands on the ball as she shoots – as well as that of her teammates, taking mental notes in order to fine-tune her technique, theirs, or both the next time the particular skill is practiced. By contrast, when scrimmaging or playing in an actual game, she's likely to spend most of her time participating – throwing herself into the moment and doing whatever is most effective. Of course, at times she may shift back to noticing, especially when sitting on the bench and watching the game from the sidelines. However, when on the court, she's likely to be in what researchers call a state of flow (Csikszentmihalyi, 2008), moving almost reflexively and instinctually in response to the quick movements of her teammates and opponents.

Coming back to mindfulness practice, you can either notice what's going on within or outside of you as a basketball player might when doing drills in practice, or you can dive entirely into the moment as if you are on the court, immersed in an important game. Either way, the goal is to practice mindfulness without judgment and without distraction. When judgmental or distracting thoughts emerge (as they do for all of us), simply notice these thoughts and then gently redirect your attention back to your practice. For instance, you might say to yourself, "Ah, yes, I'm thinking about my to-do list again, let me come back to noticing my breath."

Although certainly not comprehensive, the following is a list of some examples of different ways to engage in both kinds of practice, whether you are with your kids or not. As I told Alice, I encourage you to try them all – ideally more than once each – keeping in mind that the more you practice, the more opportunities you'll find to do so. The sky really is the limit here.

Notice

Within You

- The rise and fall of your chest as you breathe
- Your feet touching the ground when sitting or walking

- The thoughts in your mind, as you watch them drift by like clouds in the sky
- Any urges to move
- Your heart beating
- The flavor of what you are eating or drinking

Outside You

- The sights around you (e.g., the trees blowing in the breeze, a butterfly fluttering by, the flame of a flickering candle)
- The sounds around you (e.g., the hum of the air conditioner, the birds chirping outside)
- The smells around you (e.g., the aroma of your food, the smell of your shampoo as you wash your hair)
- The people around you (e.g., the expressions on their faces, their body language, their tone of voice)

Participate

- Engage in a ping-pong style conversation
- Paint on canvas or paper
- Laugh out loud
- Read or listen to a book on tape
- Wash dishes by hand
- Go for a run
- Dance to music
- Play a sport or game

Mindful Living

As noted previously, mindfulness is something that you can practice no matter where you are or what you are doing. That said, you do not need to practice mindfulness every minute of the day in order to live a mindful life, nor do you need to practice for prolonged periods of time. Instead, see if you can weave brief moments of mindfulness into your day, spending a minute here and there practicing this skill. In fact, you may want to start out by practicing mindfulness when you're not with your kids. Take a moment to mindfully drink your coffee in the morning – or even just the first sip – noticing its flavor as you drink it before you move on to packing lunches and cleaning up the breakfast dishes. Or, while walking the dog, take 30 seconds to feel your feet hit the pavement before listening to the news or calling a friend. Even these bite-sized moments can make a big difference over time. Indeed, each time you practice mindfulness – whether for just a second, 30 seconds, or more – the stronger your muscles for tuning into the present become.

Remember, there's no need to practice perfectly. Even the most seasoned mindfulness practitioners get distracted by thoughts, sounds, urges, judgments, etc., when practicing. This means that when you get distracted, there's no need to judge yourself for these natural wanderings of the mind or conclude that you aren't "good" at mindfulness. As noted previously, all that's needed is awareness of the fact that your mind has wandered, followed by a compassionate shift of your attention back to the present.

Relatedly, it's worth noting that mindfulness may come easier at some times or in some contexts than in others. For instance, it might be easier to first practice being mindful of your emotions when feeling happy or excited than when feeling intense, painful emotions such as anger, guilt, or sadness, as these unwanted emotions tend to pull for rumination about the events that prompted them. Additionally, given that most of us were socialized to focus primarily on the external world, when first getting started with this practice, you may find it easier in general to notice the external rather than the internal, even when your internal experiences are generally positive.

Mindful Parenting

With all this in mind, let's discuss how you might go about weaving mindfulness into your life as a parent. First, it's important to note that although parenting is essentially a 24/7 job, we don't have to be mindful 100 percent of the time that we are with our kids in order to reap the benefits. In fact, I doubt this would even be possible. Having said that, if you somehow find a way to be mindful in every interaction that you have with your children, please do share. I'd love to know how you do it!

If you're at all like me, however, chances are you'll be lucky if you manage to practice mindfulness even just a fraction of the time you are with your kids. So, when ideally might you want to try to practice? In the most simplistic terms, there are two times when it may be especially helpful. The first is when the weather is pleasant (i.e., you and your kids are both mostly content), and the second is when the weather is stormy (i.e., you, your kids, or both are struggling). Now, obviously, as is the case when learning any new skill, infusing mindfulness into your life is likely going to be easiest when the atmosphere is relatively calm, especially at first. Given this, let's start by taking a look at how to incorporate mindfulness into the more peaceful parenting moments. We'll get to the stormier moments and how to approach these mindfully in Chapters 5 and 7.

First, however, it's worth noting that some of the moments listed here might not always (or ever) be relaxed in your home. If that's the case, you may want to hold off for now on practicing mindfulness in those moments that are currently challenging for you. Of course, this may change from day to day.

That said, in general, basic caregiving tasks such as feeding, diapering, dressing, and bathing kids provide natural opportunities to practice participating mindfully. Indeed, if you've ever changed a diaper when *not* mindful, you likely can think of one or two reasons why it might be helpful to participate mindfully when doing this task in particular.

Obviously, excrement isn't the only reason to approach these tasks mindfully. After all, as noted earlier in this chapter, we tend to be less effective when multitasking or distracted, and thus these tasks are likely going to take much longer if we aren't mindful when doing them. Whether missing that our kid is straining to poop while in the bath or that we are spilling a drink all over the table while pouring it, approaching these tasks mindlessly tends to leave us with even more work on our plates. Relatedly, given that kids tend to be much more helpful and cooperative when feeling connected to us, mindfully participating in these caregiving tasks can strengthen that sense of connection, thereby making these activities go much more smoothly.

Playtime is also highly conducive to mindfulness practice, although we need not always participate in our children's play or even be in the same room when they are playing. In fact, contrary to what many of us believe, whether newborns, toddlers, or tweens, our kids don't need us to direct their play or show them how each toy in front of them works. Instead, we can mindfully notice or observe our kids at play, participating mindfully only if and when they ask us to do so. And when participating in our kids' play, we can still let them take the lead while noticing and resisting any urges that we might have to dictate how their play unfolds. Similarly, whether playing with or caring for our kids, we can notice (without giving in to) any other urges we might have – including urges to check out and dive into our screens, tidy the kitchen, grab a drink, or just veg out on the couch – and then gently shift our attention back to the present moment with our kids. Again, there's no need to observe our kids playing mindfully for hours at a time. Instead, we can give them a few minutes of undivided, mindful observation or participation, and then carry on with our day – perhaps even apart from our kids. I'll talk more about this in Chapter 6.

Parenting Exercise

This week, give mindful parenting a try. For instance, when at the playground with your kids, sit on a bench and observe them playing instead of pulling out your phone or chatting with another parent. Or, when playing cards with your teen, really throw yourself into the game and resist urges to do anything but play the game. Likewise, practice engaging in basic caregiving tasks mindfully. Save the dishes in the sink for after your kids are done eating, rather than trying to wash them all before lunch is over, so that you can fully take in what's happening at the table. At bedtime, put down your phone, the laundry, or whatever else you might be tempted to pick up so you can notice when your kid is stalling and could use help brushing his teeth, putting on pajamas, or getting into bed.

Once again, as a reminder, there's no need to parent mindfully every moment that you are with your kids, nor do you need to practice for extended periods. As Alice discovered in our work together, even brief seconds or moments of mindful parenting can go a long way. After only a few weeks of practice, she reported generally feeling calmer and much more connected to her kids. She also found herself becoming more accepting of the emotions underlying her kids' most challenging behaviors (as well as her own), which left her feeling much less overwhelmed by their antics and much more confident in her ability to rise above them.

How Does It Feel?

As is the case when learning any new skill, mindful parenting can feel uncomfortable and unnatural at first, and it might be easier to practice on some days than on others. Even if your attention wanders just about every second as you try to practice, simply keep coming back to whatever you are choosing to be mindful of in that moment, and resist any urges to judge the quality of your practice both in the moment and afterward. After all, not even the greatest yogis practice mindfulness perfectly all the time. Thus, the goal when practicing is progress, not perfection, even if that progress looks variable and nonlinear – which it almost certainly will. And remember, the more often you practice, the stronger your muscles for parenting (and living) in this new, more present and attuned way will become.

References

Casey, B. J., Jones, R. M., & Hare, T. A. (2008). The adolescent brain. *Annals of the New York Academy of Sciences, 1124*, 111–126. https://doi.org/10.1196/annals.1440.010

Csikszentmihalyi, M. (2008). *Flow: The psychology of optimal experience*. Harper Perennial.

Eeles, J., & Walker, D. M. (2022). Mindfulness as taught in dialectical behavior therapy: A scoping review. *Clinical Psychology and Psychotherapy, 29*(6), 1843–1853. https://doi.org/10.1002/cpp.2764

Linehan, M. M. (2015). *DBT skills training manual* (2nd ed.). The Guilford Press.

Emotion Regulation 4

The Key to Keeping an Even Keel

As I've noted, most people who come to see me for therapy do so with the goal of "getting rid" of their anxiety. Perhaps unsurprisingly given our quick-fix society, they are often disappointed when I inform them that this isn't a goal I can or even would want to help them achieve. The reason? Like all emotions, anxiety is normal and natural and serves an adaptive, evolutionary purpose. After all, we have evolved to experience emotions – both pleasant and unpleasant ones – as they convey important messages to us and others and also motivate us to take effective and necessary action. For instance, if we didn't ever feel anxious, we'd let kids of all ages roam free, even in settings that are objectively unsafe without adult supervision. Similarly, we wouldn't impart key safety information to our children, such as to look both ways before crossing the street.

Moreover, adaptive functions aside, as much as we might want to permanently turn off painful, unwanted emotions like anxiety, this is not actually possible. In fact, research suggests that the more we try to suppress or avoid the thoughts that fuel unwanted emotions, the more frequently and intensely we are likely to experience these thoughts and feelings (Abramowitz, Tolin, & Street, 2001).

Accordingly, rather than try to help others get rid of uncomfortable emotions, I aim to help them develop new, more skillful relationships with these feelings. This is the case for both parents and non-parents alike, and is what I hope to help you do here. But before diving into how to better relate to the many undesired emotions that we face as parents, it's worth noting that even basic, universal emotions like anxiety, anger, happiness, sadness, and excitement are actually much more complex than most of us realize.

DOI: 10.4324/9781003428343-7

In fact, silly as it may sound, sometimes I like to think of emotions as being like a batch of cookies. Just as cookies are made up of ingredients that we can't always see when eating the finished product, the same is true of our emotions. Regardless of the type of cookie, most are made up of a few staple ingredients, such as flour, milk, sugar, butter, and eggs. Similarly, as Dr. Marsha Linehan notes in her Model of Emotions (Linehan, 2015), each of our emotions is made up of a handful of ingredients. And as is the case when baking cookies, tweaking even just one of these ingredients can yield a very different result. With this in mind, let's look at the basic components that make up each of our emotions, whether positive or negative. From there, we'll discuss how we can use this complexity to our advantage to help us better regulate our moods.

Key Ingredients

Like the wet and dry ingredients that, when combined, give way to cookie dough, there are two sets of ingredients that make up each emotion. The first set can be thought of as factors that have the potential to kick off an emotion. I'll call these the primary ingredients. They include some kind of prompting event or potential emotional trigger, thoughts or interpretations about the prompting event, and vulnerability factors that increase the likelihood that we'll have these thoughts or interpretations. By contrast, the second set is both dependent on and a product of the first set and includes biological changes, physical sensations, action urges, verbal and non-verbal expressions, and emotional awareness and aftereffects. Let's call these the secondary ingredients.

Sticking with the cookie analogy, when mixed together, these two sets of ingredients not only give rise to and make up a particular emotion, but they also sustain that emotion. Rest assured, however, that it's okay if all of this seems pretty confusing at the moment. Bear with me a little longer as I break this down for you and refer to Figure 4.1 to help you follow along.

The Primary Ingredients

Let's begin by taking a closer look at the primary ingredients, starting with the **prompting event**. As you might already know from experience, just about anything can function as a prompting event for an emotion. Examples of prompting events include both actual observable events, such

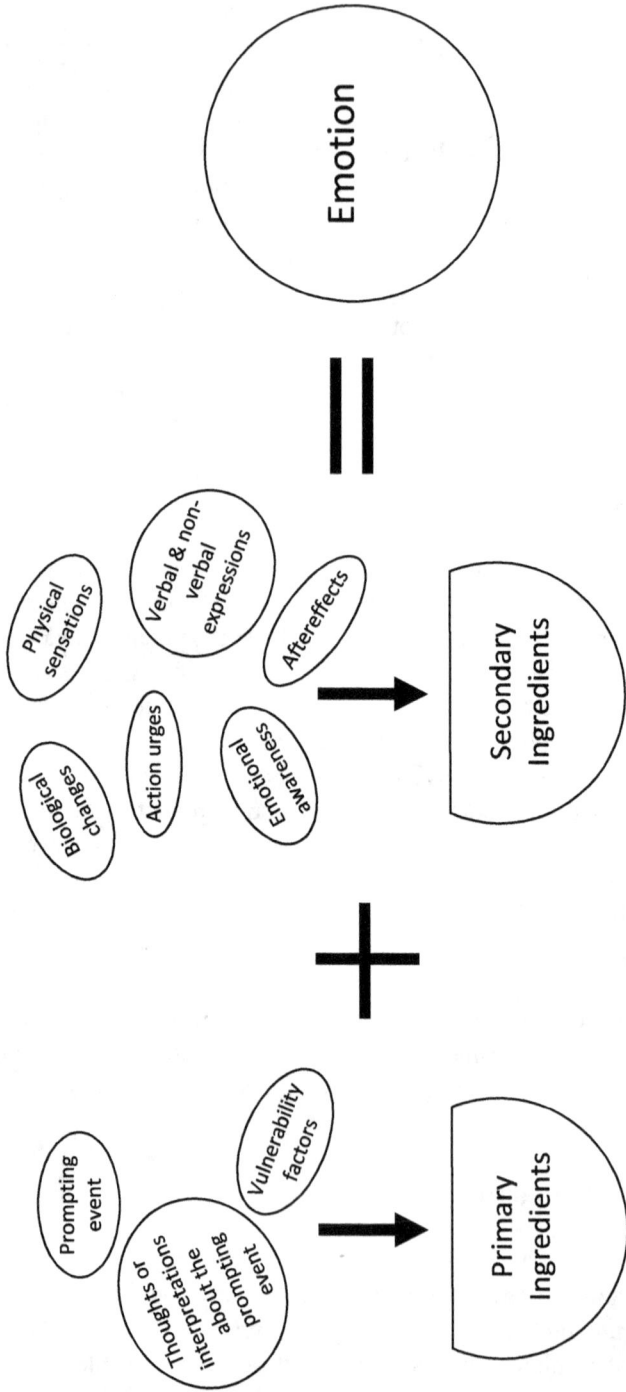

Figure 4.1 The many components that make up an emotion.

as spilling coffee all over your work blouse or an argument with one of your kids, as well as more private events, such as a memory, a thought, or even another emotion. Now of course, in order for a prompting event to have an effect on us, we must be aware of it, at least to some degree. In other words, ignorance (for as long as it lasts) really is bliss. For instance, if your kids carve their initials into your new dining room table, this may serve as a prompting event for an emotion in you when you discover their handiwork, but not beforehand. Similarly, if your kid mutters under his breath "I hate you" as you leave his room, these words may function as a prompting event for an emotion in you if, and only if, you actually hear your son utter them.

The next primary ingredient is the **thoughts or interpretations** that we have about the prompting event. Notably, these thoughts and interpretations determine if an emotion will follow a prompting event, as well as which emotion will arise. After all, how we think has an enormous impact on how we feel. For example, if you see your kids' initials carved forevermore into your table and think, "Wow, look at how neat their letters are! I didn't even know they could write their initials!" you will likely feel proud of your little ones. By contrast, if after discovering their carvings you think, "Those monsters! How could they? They destroy everything!" you are likely going to feel irate or at least something very different than pride.

Now naturally, the thoughts and interpretations that you have about a given prompting event may vary depending on the presence of certain **vulnerability factors**, which is the final primary ingredient. These vulnerability factors include experiences acquired both recently and in the distant past. Examples of more recent vulnerability factors would be not getting enough sleep the night before, having an argument with your partner immediately prior to the prompting event, feeling stressed and overwhelmed, having a cold or some other recently acquired illness or injury, feeling hungry, skipping your morning coffee, being hungover from a rare night out with friends, and so on. And chances are, you can think of many instances where you've made more negative interpretations than you would have had you not been so tired, hungry, uncomfortable, stressed, etc. I know I certainly have.

More distant vulnerability factors are experiences that we've had weeks, months, or even years ago that taint the interpretations we make in the present, thus leaving us more likely to react strongly to certain prompting events. For instance, if your parents punished you severely whenever you talked back to them, you may be more vulnerable to making negative interpretations upon hearing hurtful words such as "I hate you" coming from your son. Rather than see the feelings underlying these words, you may view them as unacceptable and disrespectful, and you may become angry as a result. Likewise, if you got a terrible case of pink eye as a kid after having forgotten to wash your hands in the bathroom, you may worry that your children will be stricken with the same condition whenever they skimp on post-toilet handwashing, and you may feel intensely anxious as a result.

The Secondary Ingredients

Now that we've covered the primary ingredients, let's move on to the secondary ingredients, which, as noted previously, include biological changes, physical sensations, action urges, verbal and non-verbal expressions, and emotional awareness and aftereffects.

Assuming an emotion has fired (i.e., a prompting event has given rise to certain interpretations, in part due to our vulnerability factors), a number of instantaneous, complex **biological changes** occur in our bodies and brains that either activate or deactivate our nervous system. When activated, as when feeling angry or anxious, we experience an *increase* in heart rate, blood pressure, temperature, perspiration, and breathing speed, all of which prepare us for action. By contrast, when deactivated, such as when feeling calm or happy, we experience a *decrease* in or *slowing down* of these processes. Noticing these biological changes is what gives rise to the bodily **sensations or feelings** that we have when an emotion has taken hold, which in turn, are typically accompanied by certain **action urges**. For example, if experiencing anger upon seeing your kids' initials carved into your table, you may sense your muscles tightening, feel as though you could explode, and have strong urges to yell at and punish your kids.

In addition, unless you have the best poker face in town or have mastered the art of channeling your inner Buddha, you will likely consciously or unconsciously **express** this emotion of anger through one or more of the following: your facial expressions, your body language, your words, your tone of voice, and/or your actions. For instance, you may frown, furrow your brows, put your hands on your hips, stomp up to your kids' playroom, and/or shout at your kids while informing them that they will not be able to use scissors ever again. At around this point, you may become **aware** that you are experiencing anger or at least some kind of strong, undesired emotion. Later, after this anger has begun to subside, you are likely to experience a number of **aftereffects**, which may manifest as changes in your thoughts, behaviors, and feelings. For instance, you may ruminate for hours about the fact that your kids carved their initials into your table, and you may find yourself moving about in a more brisk and agitated sort of way for the rest of the afternoon. You may also judge yourself for the fact that you shouted at your kids, and you may feel guilty (or some other unwanted, additional emotion) as a result.

Tweak the Recipe

As noted earlier, swapping out even just one of these ingredients for another can lead to an entirely different emotional response. And what's neat about the fact that there are many different components to any given emotion is that there are just as many points for intervention. Thus, in order to alter or dial down the intensity of an emotion, you simply need to target any one of the ingredients that make up that emotion and replace it with something else; though what, specifically, you'll want to sub in will depend on which ingredient you are aiming to tweak. For example, if I become angry whenever my kids scream at the top of their lungs, then I might decide to change the prompting event itself by popping in earplugs to block out some of the sound or by stepping out of the room when the shrieking gets past a comfortable volume. Alternatively, if my kids' screaming only prompts anger in me when I am sleep deprived and hungry, then I might aim to decrease these vulnerability factors by getting more sleep and by eating more frequent and filling meals and snacks.

With this in mind, let's start by discussing how to modify the primary ingredients, given that it's this first set that determines whether an emotion is going to fire in the first place. Since the secondary ingredients are essentially a byproduct of the primary ones and only manifest once an emotion has fired, we'll cover strategies for altering these remaining ingredients subsequently, in the next chapter. Stated differently, whereas this chapter will focus on strategies for regulating our emotional experience both preemptively and after an emotion has arisen (see Figure 4.2 for an overview of these skills), the distress tolerance chapter, which comes next, will focus exclusively on navigating emotions once they are already in full swing.

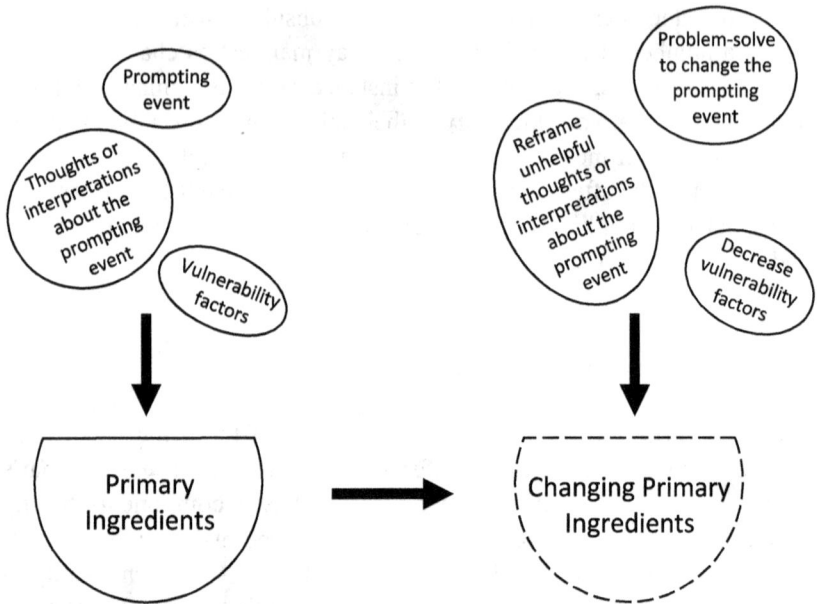

Figure 4.2 Changing the primary ingredients that make up an emotion.

Problem-Solve to Change the Prompting Event

One of the simplest ways to preempt or change an emotion is to eliminate the prompting event. Obviously, this is often easier said than done, but it can sometimes be more doable than we realize. For instance, Milo, a former patient of mine, would "fly off the handle" whenever his older children hit his youngest. After validating how upsetting these sibling scuffles can be, he and I spent some time trying to figure out when, exactly, this hitting was occurring. A week later, Milo reported back that the hitting seemed to happen whenever he was on his phone while his kids were playing next to him. Accordingly, we decided to see what would happen if he were to put his phone in another room before heading to the playroom to be with his kids and observe them at play. To our delight, Milo returned the following week and exclaimed that the hitting stopped entirely, thereby eliminating the main prompting event for his anger. In other words, identifying and then removing the cause for the prompting event leading to anger extinguished the anger altogether.

Admittedly, changing a prompting event is not always so easy. Indeed, Milo was lucky in that his kids only seemed to hit in his presence when his attention was captured by his phone. For many families, however, hitting (as well as other challenging behaviors) can happen just about any time, even when we are fully present and engaged.

This was the case for Suriya, whose bold, 22-month-old would hit her older brother in plain sight, even when she was sitting on Suriya's lap. And to Suriya's dismay, there didn't appear to be a reliable cause for this hitting, even though the hitting reliably prompted anger in her. Consequently, we decided that Suriya would shadow her girl closely whenever she and her brother were in the same room together. The plan was for her to expect that her toddler might try to hit her brother *at all times*, and for her to be close by in order to calmly and gently block these attempts, whenever possible, thereby removing the prompting event altogether. We also agreed that she would have her kids spend time in separate spaces whenever she could not watch her daughter so closely, no matter how much they begged to play together. And although shadowing her daughter and repeatedly setting and holding these limits required *a lot* of work and patience initially, within a few weeks, her daughter's attempts to hit subsided drastically, and eventually, became a thing of the past.

A final way to target a prompting event is to problem-solve *with* your kids in order to find a mutually agreeable solution. For instance, Dalia used to get upset whenever her teens would pull out their phones at the dinner table, especially since she had let them know on numerous occasions that she did not appreciate their phones' dinnertime appearances. Although dinner always started out screen-free, there seemed to be an inevitable ping that would leave one (or all) of her kids reaching for their phones midway through just about every meal. After many weeks of this, Dalia finally asked her kids to join her for a family meeting to brainstorm *together* what could be done about the dinnertime interruptions. Notably, while it was plain that she could just take away her kids' phones before dinner – or even altogether – she knew that nothing would tank her relationship with her kids more than if she were to come between them and their phones. Accordingly, after letting them know that she was continuing to feel angry and hurt by their mealtime phone use, Dalia invited her kids to share their ideas for addressing the issue, making it clear that all ideas were welcome, no matter how far-fetched.

Once all ideas were on the table, they discussed each one together, sharing what they liked and didn't like about the items, one by one. Ultimately, they concluded as a group that it would feel best if everyone, including Dalia and her partner, were to put their phones on silent before dropping them into a basket just outside of the kitchen, where they would stay for the duration of every dinner. They also agreed that if this didn't seem to work after giving it a try, they would go back to the drawing board and try out the next most promising solution. This second problem-solving session turned out not to be needed, however, as they all agreed a few nights in that not only did the phone basket eliminate the prompting event for Dalia's anger, but it also gave way to more meaningful (and at times playful) conversations that hadn't seemed possible when their phones were so close at hand.

Reframe Unhelpful Thoughts

Obviously, removing the prompting event for a given emotion is not always an option, especially when you are a parent. No matter how old your children are, they are likely going to act or react in ways that sometimes push your buttons. Whether it's your toddler throwing a tantrum in the middle of the mall or your teen slamming her door and screaming, "F&!@ you!" because you won't let her go to an unsupervised party, sometimes being a parent requires setting and holding necessary limits while facing the music (also known as your child's wrath). Needless to say, these blasts from our kids can sometimes serve as prompting events for our own anger, guilt, anxiety, disappointment, etc. And yet, regardless of the circumstances, the only thing fully in our control in moments like these is how *we* respond to our kids' outbursts and unwanted behaviors. Thankfully, although we can't always remove prompting events themselves, we can make the conscious choice to alter how we view these challenging moments, thus making it less likely that we'll experience or give in to unhelpful emotional urges that might lead us to act in ways we'll later regret.

After all, as discussed previously, our thoughts have an enormous impact on how we feel and help determine whether a given emotion will fire. Consequently, recognizing the unhelpful thoughts we have about prompting events (especially those involving our kids) and reframing these thoughts to be both more realistic and helpful can drastically shift our emotional experience. And though changing what's on our minds is certainly anything but easy, the process of restructuring unhelpful thoughts can be broken down into three, relatively straight-forward steps adapted from cognitive-behavioral therapy (see Beck, 2021; Gillihan, 2018 for more on this): 1) recognize unhelpful thoughts; 2) get curious about these thoughts; and 3) create alternative, more useful thoughts.

Beginning with step one, when it comes to catching unhelpful thoughts, practice really does make progress, as simply paying attention to our thoughts can increase awareness of unhelpful thoughts that previously flew under the radar. Thus, know that you may not always be able to identify these thoughts when faced with a prompting event and a strong emotional response, especially at first. Oftentimes, this is because these thoughts appear so rapidly and give rise to such intense emotions that these feelings become just about all we can see. In fact, it may appear as though some emotions arise entirely on their own, devoid of any thoughts. However, as noted earlier, all emotions are made up of the same basic components, including thoughts and interpretations, even if we are unable to consciously spot these cognitions.

Fortunately, the more we practice looking for the unhelpful thoughts that are getting in our way, the better we become at identifying them. So, the next time you find yourself feeling an undesired emotion in response to a prompting event, take a moment to consider what thoughts might have precipitated the emotion. For instance, might the irritation you feel in response to your daughter's stalling at bedtime be driven, at least in part, by the thought that she's disrespectful and never listens? Chances are, the more you look out for these kinds of thoughts, the stronger your inner thought detector will become.

Before moving on to step two, it's worth noting that this first step can be painful at times. After all, it's much easier to conclude that we're upset with our kids because of something *they* did wrong, rather than to acknowledge that our anger likely has every bit as much (if not more) to do with our own not-so-pleasant thoughts about our kids. With this in mind, I want to stress that no matter how terrible they may sound, the unhelpful thoughts that you have about your kids and their behavior do *not* make you a bad parent. All parents have some variation of these thoughts at times, even if they would never admit this publicly. So, there's no need to berate yourself for having these thoughts. Instead, I encourage you to take a moment to mindfully notice these thoughts when they show up – without judging yourself for having them – so that you can see them for what they are: thoughts. For example, you might say, "Ah, I'm having the thought that he's such a bully".

From here, it's time to move on to step two, which involves getting curious about the unhelpful thought in order to better understand its origin and impact on you. Here are two overarching questions to get you started, as well as some follow-ups for each of these:

1) **What's the evidence for and against the thought?**
   - Is the thought factually true? In other words, would it hold up in a court of law?
   - What evidence, if any, *doesn't* support the thought?
   - What other possible explanations might account for the undesired behavior (i.e., the prompting event)? For instance, might the behavior be a cry for help?
2) **How is the thought serving you?**
   - How does the thought make you feel?
   - Is the thought motivating you to act in ways that are consistent with who you want to be as a parent and person?

As you reflect on each of these questions and consider your answers to them, it's worth keeping in mind that our thoughts are just thoughts; they aren't facts. Relatedly, thanks to the negativity bias discussed in Chapter 2, the thoughts we have about our kids often skew toward the negative. Ergo, just because you are having the thought that your kid is a bully doesn't mean that's actually the case.

In fact, if the prompting event that triggered this thought (i.e., that your son is a bully) was seeing your son yell at his teammate for not paying attention and missing what could have been the game-winning catch, there's a good chance this thought would not hold up in a court of law. In other words, if argued before a panel of jurors, the jurors would likely disagree with your conclusion that this one instance makes your son a bully. Indeed, the jurors might point out that in order for someone to be considered a bully, they must deliberately antagonize vulnerable individuals repeatedly, not just in a single moment of frustration. They might even note that your son ended up giving the kid who messed up a friendly pat on the shoulder, suggesting that your son is actually friends with his teammate and not a bully. They might also draw your attention to the fact that some of your son's coaches and other teammates also shouted when the catch was missed, indicating that emotions were running high for all and that it was likely difficult to inhibit the urges that accompanied these strong feelings given the stressful circumstances. Sure, your son (and the rest of his team) might benefit from help in this regard, but that doesn't make him a bully.

As for the remaining questions, thinking of your son as a bully probably doesn't serve you all that well or leave you wanting to act in a kind and loving way toward him. If anything, this thought likely makes you feel like shouting at your son, while stirring up a good amount of anger and disappointment within you. In other words, this thought is neither realistic nor helpful.

Keeping these answers in mind, it's time to move on to step three, which involves using these answers to generate an alternative thought that is both more factual and useful. What, specifically, this new thought looks like is up to you. For instance, you might say, "Wow, he was really frustrated there and clearly lost his cool, but it seems as though he realized this and tried to repair any damage done." Or, you might say, "It looks like he might need some help managing his anger when he's on the field. He clearly cares about his teammates and likely feels bad that he yelled at one of them." Or you might come up with something else entirely. The goal is simply to see if you can generate a new thought that leaves you feeling a little better than the original thought did.

It's worth noting, however, that this reframing process can feel rather tedious and cumbersome at first. In fact, when done in therapy, the process is usually carried out with pen and paper, and it can sometimes take an entire session just to restructure a single thought. That said, whether you choose to challenge your thoughts on paper or simply in your head, know that the process will likely start to feel more natural with practice. Until then, Table 4.1 summarizes the three steps to reframing an unhelpful thought so that you can refer back to it as needed.

Table 4.1 Steps for reframing an unhelpful thought.

---

1) Recognize the unhelpful thought.
2) Get curious about the thought.
   - What's the evidence for and against the thought?
     - Is it factually true? What evidence doesn't support it? Might there be an alternative explanation?
   - How is the thought serving you?
     - Does it make you feel better or worse? Does it help you be the parent you want to be?
3) Create an alternative, more useful thought.

Additionally, it's important to highlight that we're not aiming to create a thought that's glowingly positive or dismissive of the prompting event, as would be the case if you told yourself, "It's okay for him to yell at his teammates – he obviously just wants his team to win and is trying to help them do just that." The reason? In addition to condoning your son's behavior, repeatedly generating overly positive, alternative thoughts such as this could lead to what's called "toxic positivity" (Goodman, 2022), which can be harmful as it involves a denial of reality (i.e., the opposite of acceptance). As you know from the previous chapter, rejecting reality rarely, if ever, serves us well.

A final caveat: Not all thoughts are amenable to restructuring, and some may even intensify in response to efforts to restructure them. This is especially true for the "what if" questions that often leave us feeling anxious and uncertain, such as, "What if she never makes friends?" or "What if he gets hurt or sick while at camp?" As a result, I recommend refraining from trying to restructure these kinds of thoughts and, instead, simply treating them as possibilities, rather than eventualities. After all, there's no way to know exactly what the future will hold, so we can accept that our feared outcomes *might* happen when these thoughts arise, thereby increasing our tolerance for uncertainty in the process.

Relatedly, if you find that your attempts to restructure a given thought aren't working for you, feel free to instead mindfully observe the thought when it pops up, almost as though you are waving hello to it when you see it, before shifting your attention back onto the present. And know that it's okay if this thought keeps coming up again and again. Although our thoughts do impact how we feel, there's no need for them to dictate what we do or don't do. Thus, even if the thought "he is being such a bully" continues to buzz around in your head, leaving you feeling angry and disappointed in your son, you can still choose to act lovingly toward him and give him a warm hug after his game. After all, our thoughts are just thoughts; we don't have to let them control us.

Decrease Emotional Vulnerability

Given that we may not always be able to directly change prompting events or our thoughts or interpretations about these events, we can aim (when possible) to decrease the number of factors that are likely to make us more vulnerable to experiencing challenging thoughts and emotions if and when our kids melt down or act out in some way. After all, while not all vulnerability factors fall under our influence, how our bodies feel, which – barring a chronic or acute illness or injury – is largely determined by the day-to-day choices we make, can have an enormous impact on the emotions and thoughts we experience when faced with a potential prompting event.

Indeed, when sleep deprived, hungry, overstuffed from a large meal, hung over, or restless or lethargic due to a lack of exercise, our threshold for what might kick off an undesired emotion in us tends to be much lower. Accordingly, one of the simplest ways to reduce our vulnerability to painful emotions is to prioritize our bodies' basic needs. That said, most of the people I know (myself included) regularly tend to neglect one or more of these vital aspects of self-care, especially when stressed or overwhelmed. So, let's get back to the basics and discuss three ways to care for our bodies in order to reduce our vulnerability to painful emotions.

1) **Fuel Our Bodies**

   Like a car, our bodies need fuel in order to function properly. Eating healthy, nutritious food and drinking water at a regular cadence can go a long way toward helping both our bodies and our minds, provided that we are not consuming too little or too much. In addition, some of us need certain medications in order to function at our best, whether for short periods of time (e.g., antibiotics) or over the long haul (e.g., insulin). Taking these as prescribed is key, as they likely won't do all that much good if taken haphazardly. It's also important to avoid fueling our bodies with substances that alter our moods, or at least to use these in moderation. This means abstaining from or limiting our consumption of alcohol, non-prescription drugs, and very sugary foods, as these can all greatly impact our ability to regulate our emotions, not only while under their influence but also long afterward.

2) **Move Our Bodies**

Once fueled, moving or exercising our bodies on a daily or almost daily basis is critical for our overall well-being and mood regulation. And while some movement is certainly better than none, as is the case with food, it's best to make sure that we aren't under- or over-doing our dose of exercise. Instead, we want to engage in whatever type, amount, and intensity of exercise feels right for our bodies and fitness goals, keeping in mind that this may vary from person to person, as well as over time. As such, running, swimming, tai-chi, yoga, hockey, Pilates, biking, walking, rowing, weightlifting, etc., are all fair game here. And if exercising is new for you or something that's been on the backburner ever since you had kids, know that it's okay to gradually build up here, even if it takes a while to get to the Centers for Disease Control and Prevention (CDC) recommendation of at least 150 minutes of moderate-intensity physical activity (or 75 minutes of vigorous-intensity physical activity) per week (CDC, 2023). Be sure to give yourself credit for whatever exercise you are able to fit in each day, even if it's just time spent chasing your toddler around the house or playing soccer with your older kids in the backyard.

3) **Rest Our Bodies**

As any overtired parent of a newborn can tell you, our bodies also need rest in the form of restorative sleep. What's this, you ask??? I know, I know – I too have had periods where the thought of getting the 7 or more hours of sleep per night that the CDC recommends for most adults (CDC, 2024) feels every bit as far-fetched as becoming Queen of the United States of America. And yet, often this is because my husband and I stay up way too late binge-watching our new favorite TV show night after night, thus willingly (and foolishly I'll add) choosing to forgo meeting this vital need. Unfortunately, this decision almost always comes back to bite me the next day when I'm with my kids, as

I've found that I'm not only more likely to get angry or frustrated with them when sleep deprived but also not as well equipped to inhibit the unhelpful urges that accompany these feelings. Thus, although I sometimes choose otherwise, I do make a conscious effort to aim for at least 7 hours of sleep on most nights. Having said that, while I realize that the thought of too much sleep might seem even more laughable to you than the concept of restorative sleep, it's worth noting that there is such a thing as too much sleep (yes, even for us parents) and that this, too, can negatively impact our ability to regulate our emotions. In other words, as is the case for fueling and moving our bodies, when it comes to sleep, the Goldilocks approach is what we ideally want to aim for: not too little and not too much, but instead, just the right amount.

Obviously, we aren't the only ones who benefit from fueling, moving, and resting our bodies. As you've likely gathered from your own experience, giving kids time, space, and support to meet these needs can greatly reduce their emotional vulnerability as well. That said, I don't believe we can (or should) control whether our kids eat the food we serve, run around the playground, or close their eyes when we turn off the lights and say goodnight. This is because at the end of the day, how much our kids eat, move, and sleep is really up to them. Our job is merely to provide the context for them to meet each of these needs in whatever ways they choose.

Of course, how our own bodies feel is not always within our control either, even for those of us who never miss a beat when it comes to caring for ourselves in these ways. Likewise, we may not always be physically capable of fueling, moving, or resting our bodies, even if we're usually committed to doing so. For instance, when sick with a chronic or acute illness, it may be difficult to adhere to some or all of these self-care strategies.

In fact, just as not all prompting events or thoughts about these can be changed, the same is true of vulnerability factors. Indeed, physical illnesses and injuries are vulnerability factors in and of themselves, and we certainly cannot always prevent these. Similarly, discovering that your roof needs an unexpected and expensive repair, a heated argument with your partner, a stressful day at work, traumatic events that happened in the distant past, and so on are all examples of vulnerability factors that may be somewhat or largely out of our control. Of course, we may be able to acquire and use skills to help us better cope with these kinds of stressors, but the reality is that most of us carry at least a few vulnerability factors with us wherever we go. Reminding ourselves of this can be helpful, as these vulnerability factors can easily color the thoughts and interpretations we make when faced with a potential prompting event, thus increasing the likelihood that an unwanted emotion will fire.

Parenting Exercise

Over the next few weeks, try out each of these emotion regulation skills. Problem-solve prompting events that are within your control, reframe whatever unhelpful thoughts arise about your kids, and aim to rest, fuel, and move your body in a way that feels good for you. Remember, it's okay if using these skills feels awkward or unnatural at first. It's also okay if you forget to use these skills at times or even sometimes consciously make the choice to not use them. Either way, the key is to notice how you feel when you are using these skills consistently and when you aren't. Chances are, the more you use them, the better you'll feel. Having said that, if you find it difficult to use these skills or if other vulnerability factors are getting in your way (e.g., chronic depression, anxiety, insomnia), I'd recommend turning to the Resources section of the Support Material for this book (www. routledge.com/9781032544946) and looking for a mental health professional who can help you navigate these issues. Whether working with a therapist or on our own, addressing whatever's making it difficult for us to be the parents we want to be is truly one of the best investments we can make – not only for ourselves but also for our children.

References

Abramowitz, J. S., Tolin, D. F., & Street, G. P. (2001). Paradoxical effects of thought suppression: a meta-analysis of controlled studies. *Clinical Psychology Review, 21*(5), 683–703. https://doi.org/10.1016/S0272-7358(00)00057-X

Beck, J. S. (2021). *Cognitive behavior therapy: Basics and beyond* (3rd ed.). The Guilford Press.

Centers for Disease Control and Prevention. (2023, December 20). *Adult activity: An overview.* https:// www.cdc.gov/physical-activity-basics/guidelines/adults.html

Centers for Disease Control and Prevention. (2024, May 15). *About sleep.* https://www.cdc.gov/sleep/about/index.html#cdcreference_3

Gillihan, S. J. (2018). *Cognitive behavioral therapy made simple: 10 strategies for managing anxiety, depression, anger, panic and worry.* Althea Press.

Goodman, W. (2022). *Toxic positivity: Keeping it real in a world obsessed with being happy.* TarcherPerigee.

Linehan, M. M. (2015). *DBT skills training manual* (2nd ed.). The Guilford Press.

Distress Tolerance

5

The Secret to Surviving Emotional Storms

But how do we refrain from giving in to the unhelpful urges that our most intense and challenging feelings pull for? That's where the distress tolerance skills we'll discuss in this chapter come into play. Again, as parents, we won't always be able to change the prompting events, unhelpful thoughts, and vulnerability factors (discussed in the previous chapter) that give rise to painful emotions in us. Fortunately, however, we can always target the other components that make up these emotions (i.e., the secondary ingredients) in order to reduce the likelihood that these feelings will hijack our interactions with our kids. As a reminder, the secondary ingredients consist of biological changes, physical sensations, action urges, verbal and non-verbal expressions, and emotional awareness and aftereffects. Also, as stated previously, the advantage of this complexity is that it allows for many different ways to shake things up so that we can better tolerate our distress, rather than allow it to make things worse for ourselves and our kids. So, with this in mind, let's get to the skills (an overview of which can be found in Figure 5.1), beginning with those that target the biological changes and physical sensations that we experience when feeling a strong emotion.

The CARE Skills: Skills for Dampening Emotional Arousal

The skills that I will cover now for dousing the flames of emotional arousal are some of my favorite skills of all time.[1] Essentially, these are skills for

---

1 Those of you who are familiar with DBT will recognize these as the TIP skills, which were developed by Dr. Marsha Linehan as part of her comprehensive treatment for emotion

DOI: 10.4324/9781003428343-8

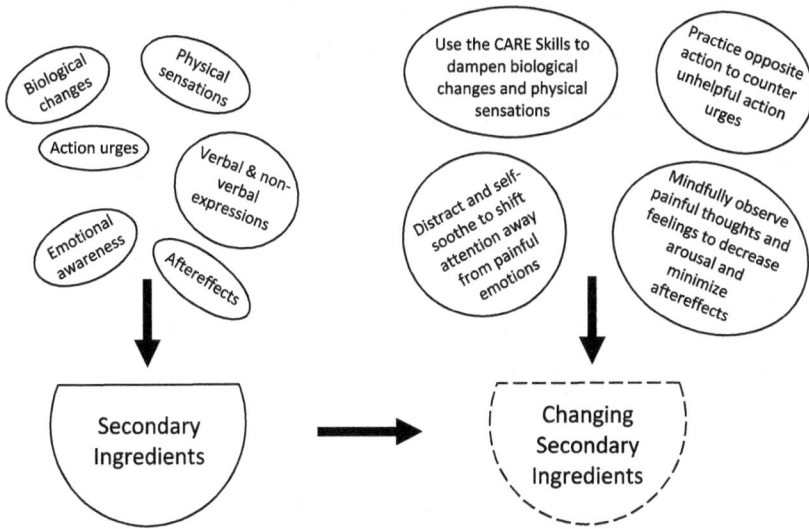

Figure 5.1 Changing the secondary ingredients that make up an emotion.

rapidly modulating the biological changes that, along with the other ingredients outlined in Chapter 4, comprise strong emotions. What's neat about these skills is that they can be used anytime, anywhere, and can cool intense emotions within seconds by activating the part of the nervous system that helps us relax (the parasympathetic nervous system), while also decreasing activity in the part of the nervous system that increases arousal and activates the body's fight-or-flight response (the sympathetic nervous system). In case it helps, you can remember these skills with the acronym CARE. After all, when strong emotions are on board, we need to proceed with *care* in order to make sure that we don't succumb to the whims of our emotions. Here's what CARE stands for:

Cool with ice
Activate your body
Relax your muscles
Exhale slowly

dysregulation (Linehan, 2015). While I am a huge fan of these skills, I've always found the TIP acronym to be somewhat confusing, largely because it's a three-letter acronym for four distinct skills. As you can see, it's also a little clunky to say and recall. It stands for tipping the Temperature of your face with cold water or ice, Intense aerobic exercise, Paced breathing, and Paired muscle relaxation. Given that I believe such a fabulous set of skills deserves better, here I present the TIP skills using the acronym CARE, which I personally find easier to remember.

Again, these fast-acting skills can make painful emotions a little easier to bear, although their effects are short-lived as they aren't intended to change emotions. Given this, it's best to think of these as skills for getting our brains back so we can – once no longer emotionally hijacked – turn to other more cognitively demanding tools to help us regulate our emotional experience.

With this in mind, let's take a look at each of the skills that make up this acronym, beginning with the first one, which is even cooler than it sounds: Cool with ice. First, however, it's important to note that this skill can lead to a drastic decrease in heart rate (as you'll see below) and thus may not be appropriate for those with heart or other medical conditions, including eating disorders, or for those who take a medication, such as a beta blocker, that slows their heart rate. If any of these apply to you, please consult with a physician before attempting to use this skill.

With that said, my guess is that you are likely now wondering how ice could possibly slow the pounding of your heart in the most heated, challenging moments with your kids. Interestingly, it turns out that we are so wired for survival that when we are submerged in very cold water, our hearts slow down and stop pumping blood to our extremities in order to conserve energy and heat our cores. This is known as the mammalian dive reflex and is something we can elicit fairly easily, even if we have no intention of ever taking a polar bear plunge. All that's needed is a flexible gel ice pack applied to the face or a large bowl of very cold water that you can dunk your face into. Here are the instructions:

- If using an ice pack, wrap the pack in a damp towel or paper towel and cover your eyes, temples, and upper cheeks with it. Bend down while holding the pack to your face and holding your breath for 20–30 seconds.
- If using cold water, place a large bowl of ice water on a table and then dunk your entire face into it for 20–30 seconds while holding your breath.

And that's it! As silly as it may sound, this skill truly works wonders and can result in heart rates plummeting by 50 percent or more in less than a minute. Told you it was cool!

The next CARE skill is to Activate your body with 20 minutes of intense, aerobic exercise, such as running, swimming, cycling, brisk walking, dancing, or rowing. Ironically, although this skill involves increasing your heart rate, it, too, can dampen arousal for a number of reasons. First, intense exercise provides an outlet for discharging some of the pent-up energy we feel when emotionally charged. Instead of releasing this energy by yelling at our kids or doing something else we might regret, we can engage in a few minutes of exercise to expel this energy and allow our bodies to reset. Chances are you can think of times where you've gotten your heart rate up with exercise and then seen it come down significantly soon after ending your workout. Assuming your heart is healthy, this heart rate recovery or return to baseline happens relatively quickly following exercise, especially in contrast to what happens when experiencing a painful emotion such as anger. If you allow yourself to marinate in your anger and stew on the thoughts that accompany it, your heart rate will likely remain elevated for quite some time and may even continue to increase. In addition, intense exercise releases feel-good chemicals in our bodies called endorphins that can boost our mood and help jog us out of challenging emotions. You've likely heard the term "runner's high" – and for good reason. Whether running or engaging in some other kind of aerobic exercise, activating our bodies in this way tends to improve both our physical and mental well-being.

Next, we have Relax your muscles, which targets the tension that many of us feel in our bodies when we are emotionally upset. Instead of clenching our muscles for prolonged periods – whether consciously or unconsciously – we can utilize the skill of progressive muscle relaxation to briefly tense and release individual muscle groups one at a time. Again, as with activating your body, this may seem paradoxical at first, as it involves *tensing* your muscles, even though the goal when using this skill is to *decrease* physical tension. However, as you may already know from experience, simply relaxing your muscles is not so simple. To illustrate (for those of you who haven't given this a try before), please take a moment to relax all of your muscles right now, without doing anything else first. Just relax them. See? It's hard. Fortunately, in much the same way that a pendulum swings farther if you first pull back the weight before releasing it (in contrast to what happens if you knock the weight while at rest), it turns out that if we first tense our muscles before releasing them, we can achieve a greater sense of relaxation than if we just try relaxing them.

If you're willing, give this a try now, tensing individual muscle groups for 3–4 seconds at a time before releasing these muscles and moving on to the next muscle group. For instance, you can scrunch up all of the muscles in your face and then relax these muscles, noticing the difference as you do so. From there, you can move on to the next group of muscles (e.g., your shoulders) and then the next group of muscles (e.g., your arms) and so on, working your way through your entire body, top to bottom. Or if you're short on time, you can tense all of the muscles in your body at once for 3–4 seconds and then relax them, paying attention to how it feels to release this tension. Alternatively, you can search for guided progressive muscle relaxation exercises online and use one of the many free video or audio recordings available to guide you through the process.

Finally, the last of the four CARE skills is to Exhale slowly in order to slow your heart and relax your body. We all know that our breathing can greatly impact how we feel. In fact, chances are we have uttered and/or heard instructions to "take a deep breath" many, many times in our lives. However, it turns out that when we take a big breath in (as most of us do in response to this instruction), we actually speed up our hearts and heighten arousal even further. This is because our heart rates increase with each inhalation and decrease with each exhalation. Similarly, when we breathe quickly, as many of us do when emotionally charged, our heart rates also quicken. Thus, when emotionally heated, one way to dampen arousal is to take a normal breath in and a long and slow breath out. We can even slow this process down further by briefly holding our breath after each exhalation before taking the next inhalation. For instance, we can breathe in for 3–4 seconds, breathe out for 7–8 seconds, and then hold our breath for 3–4 seconds before moving on to the next breath (as depicted in Figure 5.2). Or if you know a different breathing technique, such as triangle breathing or box breathing, feel free to use that. You can also experiment with different counts until you find what works best for you. All that matters is that your exhalation is longer than your inhalation.

Having said that, if you haven't tried breathing in this way before, I encourage you to give it a shot now for at least a few breath cycles, keeping in mind that it may feel unnatural at first. Indeed, this skill really does take a good amount of practice to master, which is why I usually recommend practicing it at least once per day for 10 minutes at a time when first learning it. I also advise folks to begin by practicing this skill when feeling calm before moving on to trying this skill when distressed, as it can be challenging to focus on our breathing when emotionally charged, especially if we aren't used to breathing in this way. Luckily, however, the more you practice

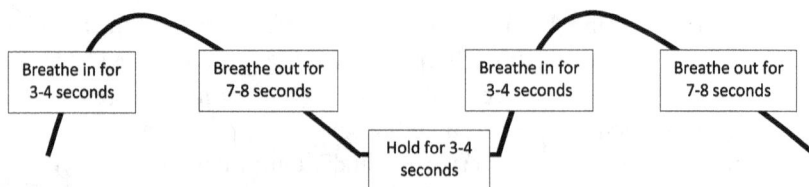

| Breathe in for 3-4 seconds | Breathe out for 7-8 seconds | | Breathe in for 3-4 seconds | Breathe out for 7-8 seconds |

Hold for 3-4 seconds

Figure 5.2 How to practice the skill of exhaling slowly.

exhaling slowing when relaxed, the more likely it is that muscle memory for this new way of breathing will kick in when feelings are running high so that you can cool your temper before you lose it with your kids.

Opposite Action: A Skill for Addressing Unhelpful Action Urges and Body Language Changes

The next skill we'll discuss is another one of my favorites and is designed to target the unhelpful action urges that we sometimes have when experiencing challenging emotions. It's called opposite action by some and exposure by others,[2] and it's a powerful skill for moments when our emotions misfire (or fire too intensely) or give way to action urges that are counterproductive to our goals (Linehan, 2015). To be sure, our emotions are very important and provide valuable information to us and others, and we certainly don't ever want to ignore or suppress what we're feeling. In fact, there are many instances where it would be harmful to *not* act on our emotion urges. However, as discussed previously, our emotions sometimes lead us to act in ways that aren't effective or consistent with how we want to show up in the world or with our kids; and it's at these times that opposite action can be helpful. With that said, let's talk about what opposite action actually entails.

In much the same way that you get up in the morning to care for your kids or get ready for work even when you're tired and feel like staying in bed all day, opposite action involves doing the opposite of what you *feel* like doing. So, for instance, if you want to tell your elementary school-age kids that they can't play on the monkey bars because you're anxious and fear that they'll fall and get hurt, opposite action might involve allowing your kids to play on the monkey bars given that doing so is considered a developmentally appropriate, reasonable risk that most parents are willing to let their same-age kids take. Similarly, if you're disappointed that your teen got a C on his biology test and you feel pulled to ground him until he does better or

---

2 For those of you who are familiar with DBT, you may be wondering why this skill is in a chapter on distress tolerance, when DBT presents it as an emotion regulation skill. As noted previously, this chapter is focused exclusively on skills that we can use once an emotion has already fired, whereas the emotion regulation chapter consists of skills that target what I like to think of as the prerequisites for an emotion firing. Additionally, given that opposite action essentially involves doing the exact opposite of what a given emotion is pulling for, we can't really practice it in the absence of that emotion. In other words, opposite action is a skill that we can use only after an emotion has fired. Further, while emotions do sometimes change when acting opposite to the urges that accompany them, that's not always the case. Accordingly, I believe that the goal of opposite action is not to change a given emotion, but instead to learn that you can tolerate that emotion and still act in ways that align with who you want to be as a parent and person.

lecture him about how disappointed you are, opposite action might involve letting him know that you love him no matter what grades he gets and that you want to support him academically in whatever ways he would find most helpful. It might also involve problem-solving with him to come up with a plan to help him do better next time, rather than insisting he follow a plan of your own. Likewise, if you feel angry upon seeing your four-year-old yank her younger sister by the hair and notice urges to shout at or punish her for this, you can act opposite to these angry urges by calmly and non-judgmentally discussing what happened and asking your daughter how you might be able to help her the next time she feels like hurting her sister.

No matter the emotion, the key is to make sure that you are acting *entirely* opposite to the action urges that the emotion is pulling for (assuming that acting on these urges would be unhelpful or ineffective). Otherwise, you'll likely only reinforce the belief that painful emotions are intolerable unless you give into one or more of the urges that accompany them. In other words, if you allow your kids to play on the monkey bars but hover next to them the entire time and repeatedly tell them to be careful while scrunching up your face and wringing your hands, you aren't practicing opposite action, at least not all the way. By the same token, if you say all the right things to your kids in a cold and disapproving tone while scowling at them and folding your arms, that's not really acting opposite to the emotions of disappointment or anger either.

Thus, when practicing opposite action, it's important to pay attention to each of your behaviors, including your actions, your words, your tone of voice, your facial expressions, and your body language. Then, all that's needed is to do the opposite of what your emotion is pulling for you to do. For instance, if you tend to frown or clench your fists when angry with your kids, consider slightly raising the corners of your lips to form a small smile and keeping your palms relaxed and open as part of your opposite action practice. In DBT, this is known as half-smiling and willing hands (Linehan, 2015).

Again, it's okay to feel anxious, disappointed, angry, or whatever other emotion you are feeling when acting opposite to it. If that emotion decreases with opposite action, that's great! For example, maybe your anxiety goes down as you watch your kids cross the monkey bars and maneuver around the playground, in part because you realize that they're safer and more competent than you believed them to be.

Having said that, sometimes emotions stay elevated even after practicing opposite action for a while, in which case we need to do some detective work to figure out what this means.

One possibility is that the emotion is actually appropriate for the situation and that it's worth heeding the urges that accompany it. For instance, if your anxiety remains high as you watch your toddler have one close call after another on the playground, you might want to look around to see if other kids her age are on the same play structures. And if while doing so you happen to notice a sign that says "intended for ages 6+" then opposite action likely wouldn't be the best skill for the situation. Instead, you'd probably want to problem-solve the prompting event by moving your daughter to a more age-appropriate section of the playground.

Alternatively, it may be that your emotion isn't budging because you're unknowingly feeding it by giving in to some (even if not all) of the urges that come with it. For example, if your older kids are doing just fine on the monkey bars but you continue to spot them as they make their way across, you're essentially telling your brain that they're at greater risk than they actually are. As a result, your anxiety will almost invariably stay high.

A final possibility is simply that the emotion is going to remain high for a while, despite practicing opposite action all the way in a situation that warrants it. For instance, maybe you feel intensely anxious the entire time your kids are on the playground, even though they are clearly capable of playing safely on it. If so, rest assured that this prolonged, elevated emotional state is not a bad thing as it allows you to discover that you can feel intensely anxious about your children's safety without having to prevent them from engaging in developmentally normative play. In instances such as these, learning that you can tolerate painful emotions and still show up as you want to for your kids can be immensely impactful. Sure, it might not feel good if an unwanted emotion remains high, but there's really no better way to learn that your feelings don't have to call the shots than if a challenging emotion that's pulling for unhelpful actions stays every bit as intense as it once was while you continue acting opposite to it.

Indeed, recognizing that we can choose to *not* act on ineffective emotion urges is vital as it frees us from emotional captivity, thus enabling us to act like the calm and connected parents we want to be no matter how we're feeling on the inside. Fortunately, parenting presents us with countless opportunities to practice doing what's effective and what matters to us in spite of our strong emotions. The trick is in being able to see these moments for the gifts that they are instead of dreading them or trying to ensure that we never encounter such moments again. This shift in perspective allows us to act in ways that strengthen our muscles for tolerating distress while also modeling for our children the power that lies in being able to feel intense emotions without letting them govern our every move. And though you may not always remember to view challenging moments as golden opportunities to practice relating differently to uncomfortable emotions, I encourage you to try to adopt this view whenever possible.

Distract and Self-Soothe: Skills for Shifting Attention Away From Emotions

As is the case with life in general, parenting is bound to be filled with moments that feel intolerable at times – both for us and for our kids. In these moments, pulling yourself together enough to use the skills discussed thus far might seem downright impossible. Believe me, I've been there. That's when the DBT skills of distraction and self-soothing can be especially useful (Linehan, 2015). Though certainly not rocket science, these skills can be very powerful when emotions feel all-consuming, as they remind us that there's more to life than what we're feeling in the moment. Critically, however, these skills are not intended to be used as a way to avoid emotions altogether. Instead, they are merely tools for getting a little distance or breathing room from your emotions when you feel utterly fused with them.

Although these are technically two distinct skills, I decided to introduce them together as I've found that distraction often functions as a form of self-soothing and vice versa. That said, since they are in fact separate from one another, let's take a look at the skill of distraction before moving on to self-soothing.

Distraction, as you might have guessed, involves focusing your attention on something other than the emotion itself or its components. For instance, instead of ruminating about a prompting event or devoting your energy to trying to get rid of undesired emotions or physical sensations, distraction involves allowing these thoughts, feelings, and sensations to exist in the background, while focusing your attention on something in the present.

As for what you choose to focus on, that can really be just about anything. For instance, you might choose to focus on an activity, such as a game, an art project, or a walk in the woods. Or you might focus on helping or caring for others, including one or more of your kids if you're up for doing so.

Another way to distract is to focus on something that might give rise to a different and ideally less painful emotion in you. For example, if feeling angry with your kids, you can take a quick break from parenting (assuming it's safe to do so) to read a few suspenseful pages of a novel or watch a comedy show. The opening skits from *Saturday Night Live* are usually very short and can be watched in a matter of minutes when time is of the essence. Alternatively, you can distract by generating other, hard-to-ignore sensations. For instance, you might take a hot or cold shower, walk barefoot on cold tile, eat a sour lemon, go outside on a very windy day, etc.

Whatever you choose, keep in mind that the goal when using distraction is not to get rid of intense, uncomfortable emotions, but rather to take the edge off of these feelings, thus making it a little easier to proceed skillfully in their midst. After all, there is limited mental real estate in our brains. If we can intentionally shift the spotlight of our attention to something else, then we can get a little distance from the moment and the unhelpful urges that might otherwise seem impossible to resist.

The same is true when self-soothing, which essentially is a form of distraction that involves using one of your five senses to cool (but not necessarily eliminate) hot or unwanted emotions. In other words, this skill involves soothing yourself by focusing on comforting or pleasing sights, sounds, smells, tastes, or touches. Here are some of my favorite examples of ways to self-soothe using each of the five senses:

Sight

- Go for a walk in the woods, at the beach, or in a park and notice the sights around you.
- Look at pictures of your kids when they were babies or from "happier" or "easier" times.
- Go to a museum and look at the works of art on display.
- Look at your children's artwork.
- Organize a closet, desk, or room and then admire your work.
- Go window or online shopping, even if you have no intention of buying anything.
- Sit outside and look at the sky at sunrise or sunset or at night when stars are visible.
- Watch your kids sleep or play.

Sound

- Listen to your favorite calming or uplifting music.
- Listen to waves washing ashore, rain falling, fire crackling, or a soundtrack of these sounds.
- Sit outside and listen to the birds chirping.

Taste

- Eat a piece of chocolate or a special dessert.
- Drink a warm cup of cocoa, coffee, or tea.
- Cook or order in your favorite food.

Smell

- Smell the aroma of coffee or freshly baked bread or cookies at home or in a shop.
- Go for a walk outside and take in the scent of the air, flowers, and trees around you.
- Smell an item belonging to one of your kids that has their scent on it.
- Go to a store that sells candles, lotions, body wash, etc. and smell the items one by one.

Touch

- Put a blanket in the dryer for a few minutes and then take the blanket out and wrap yourself in it.
- Stroke the hair or fur on the heads of your kid(s) or pet(s).
- Get a massage or massage a part of your body that you can reach (e.g., your feet or hands).
- Ask for a hug from a friend or loved one. (We call this hug therapy in my house.)
- Take a relaxing shower or bath and feel the warm water on your skin.
- Walk on sand barefoot.

Of course, these are just a few ideas to get you started. Feel free to try the ones that appeal to you and to experiment with other ways to soothe yourself, keeping in mind that what might be soothing for you might be very different from the things I've listed here.

Mindfully Observe Painful Thoughts and Feelings: A Skill for Decreasing Emotional Arousal and Minimizing Its Aftereffects

The final distress tolerance skill that I'll cover here is rooted in acceptance and the notion that all emotions have a natural course. In other words, even the most intense and painful emotions will eventually dissipate on their own, provided that we don't inadvertently fuel them in some way. Paradoxically, as discussed previously, one of the best ways to ensure that an emotion sticks around is to try to avoid or suppress the feeling and the thoughts that accompany it. Perhaps less surprisingly, latching onto the thoughts that make up and result from an emotion is another surefire way to fan the flames of arousal. Accordingly, sometimes the most effective approach to navigating painful thoughts and feelings is simply to mindfully notice them, without trying to judge, suppress, or cling onto these internal experiences. This mindful approach helps strengthen distress tolerance muscles while also potentially decreasing emotional arousal and minimizing any emotional aftereffects.

That said, it's worth noting that mindfully observing painful thoughts and feelings is quite possibly the most challenging way to practice mindfulness. If you haven't yet practiced mindfully noticing your external world or more pleasant internal experiences, trying to mindfully observe painful thoughts and feelings might seem akin to learning to ride a bike for the first time on a very steep incline. Thus, I encourage you to give this a try only after practicing the mindfulness exercises in Chapter 3 at least a few times. Even then, please keep in mind that there may be some moments where this skill seems almost impossible to practice. If so, know that that's to be expected, as this really is a very challenging skill to master. In fact, although I've benefited greatly many times from this skill, I'm not always able to use it effectively as I still sometimes get stuck in the rabbit hole of rumination, forgetting to come back to mindfully noticing my thoughts and feelings.

Now, assuming I haven't scared you away entirely from ever trying to use this skill, let's discuss how to go about practicing it. As you might have guessed, the good news is that the how-to for this skill is the same as that for any mindfulness practice. We simply need to tune into the thoughts or feelings we are experiencing without judging them, attaching to them, or distracting ourselves with some other task. For instance, mindfully noticing a painful emotion involves willingly surfing the wave of that feeling – however intense it may be – and observing the physical sensations that constitute it, without judging or trying to change or hold onto the experience. Of course, this is easier said than done, but that's really all there is to it.

The same goes for mindfully observing painful thoughts. Welcoming these thoughts as they come and go without trying to suppress, evaluate, or build on these thoughts is all that's needed in order to practice this skill. If it helps, you can imagine that your mind is like a creek and that your thoughts are the leaves floating down the creek. Notice each leaf as it floats downstream without trying to grab onto or follow any one leaf. Or, if you prefer, you can imagine that your mind is the sky and that your thoughts are the clouds drifting by. Let each cloud appear and then watch as these clouds drift away out of sight, one by one.

As is the case with any mindfulness practice, if you find that your mind has wandered or that you've begun judging or holding onto a given emotion or thought, simply redirect your attention back to mindfully noticing your internal experience. Rest assured that mindfulness is often described as the act of losing focus 1,000 times and shifting back to whatever you are observing 1,001 times. Stated differently, you can expect that your mind will wander when practicing mindfulness – especially when painful thoughts and feelings are on board. All that matters is that you turn your attention back to your practice each time it does.

Herculean Parenting: Using Distress Tolerance Skills to Be the Parent You Want To Be

Jake, an anxious father of four, came to see me because he was tired of getting hijacked by his emotions and "losing it" with his kids. He shared that he grew up in a cold and strict household where children were expected to be seen but not heard and where shouting and punishments were doled out for even the tiniest of infractions. Although he very much wanted to be warmer, gentler, and more emotionally attuned to his kids than his parents were with him, he found himself lashing out and/or giving his kids the silent treatment on an almost daily basis and felt as though he had no ability to regulate his behavior when upset. A part of him knew that his expectations for his kids were developmentally out-of-sync, but he struggled to let go of the unrealistic belief that kids should obey their parents and toe the line at all times, likely because that's what was expected of him and his siblings.

Accordingly, in addition to helping Jake reframe his views of his kids, our work together largely focused on learning and using distress tolerance skills for those moments when his newly acquired beliefs went out the window. After introducing each of the skills in this chapter, usually one per week, Jake's job was to practice these skills between our sessions whenever his blood started boiling – something that happened almost exclusively with his kids. And knowing his tendency to forget what he'd been learning in therapy when he was angry, he created a list of these skills that he posted around his house and set as the lock screen on his phone.

A few weeks into this work, Jake reported that his go-to skills were the CARE skills (specifically cooling with ice and exhaling slowly) and opposite action, which he said had "saved" him on numerous occasions. For example, Jake proudly recounted how he took a moment to exhale slowly and cool his face with ice after his nine-year-old tossed a ball across the kitchen, knocking over a large glass of water that then spilled all over his laptop's keyboard. Jake didn't shy away from letting me know that he was livid when this happened, as it completely fried his work computer and was clearly an "idiotic" thing to do. However, thanks to the list of distress tolerance skills that he had hung up on the fridge (which happened to be directly across from the counter island where he was sitting at the time), Jake took a few slow breaths out as he shook the water out of his keyboard and walked over to the freezer to grab an ice pack for his face. "It was wild!" he exclaimed as he described how the anger that was coursing through his body just seconds before seemed to melt away almost entirely.

Jake added that, in the past, he would have screamed at his son, who would have likely responded by shouting, "I don't care that your computer is ruined! I hate you!" Instead, his son broke the silence first, apologizing and voluntarily acknowledging that Jake was right all the times he'd previously told the kids not to throw balls in the kitchen. Although still wishing he could get his laptop back, Jake softened further with this apology, patting his son on the shoulder and letting him know, "It's okay, bud, we all make mistakes."

Not only did Jake learn that day that his anger doesn't have to control his interactions with his kids, but he also noticed that these interactions go much more smoothly when his anger isn't dictating his response. Further, Jake reflected that an angry outburst wasn't needed in order to teach his son the lesson that balls shouldn't be thrown in the kitchen. His son clearly learned that lesson on his own, without the anger or resentment that he likely would have felt had Jake forced the message upon him.

On another occasion, Jake came to our therapy session practically bursting with excitement thanks to a recent win he'd had as a result of practicing opposite action. As I mentioned earlier, Jake struggled with anxiety (especially around contamination) and met criteria for obsessive-compulsive disorder when he initially came to see me. The thought of his kids getting sick with a cold, the flu, or even something more serious was almost too much to bear when we first started meeting, and he'd been greatly restricting his children's activities long before Covid in hopes of preventing his kids from ever getting sick. Further, when his kids did something that he believed was risky, such as put a toy in their mouths that hadn't been sanitized first, Jake's anxiety would morph into anger, leading him to yell at his kids for whatever "dangerous" thing they'd been doing. Consequently, much of our work focused on acting opposite to the anxious and angry urges that he experienced in these moments.

As luck would have it, one rainy day Jake's eldest daughter asked him to take her to the gym to play basketball. Jake hated the gym as he believed it was "crawling with germs," and he usually refused to take his kids to it, even though his wife frequently did so. Thankfully, however, he recognized that this was one of those fabulous opportunities we'd been talking about to practice acting opposite to his urges to avoid things that make him anxious. Jake beamed as he told me that not only did he take his daughter to the gym, but he also played basketball with her using a ball belonging to the gym that could have been touched by anyone and was likely covered in germs. His smile grew even bigger as he told me what happened next.

Apparently, while Jake and his daughter were playing basketball, a birthday party had wrapped up in the same building, and the birthday kid and his parents came into the gym offering to share extra cupcakes. Prior to us working together, Jake would have refused the cupcakes immediately and yelled at his daughter when she begged him to change his mind. Instead, Jake thanked the family and grabbed two cupcakes from the box the birthday boy was holding – one for him and one for his daughter – with his sweaty, potentially contaminated hands. What's more, when his daughter took her unwashed finger to swipe icing off the top that she then licked, Jake decided to ride the wave of anxiety that he was feeling (rather than fight it) by joining her. They ate every last bite of their cupcakes side-by-side, hands unwashed but licked clean, while Jake privately acknowledged that they *might* get sick. And what do you know? Almost an entire week went by and they both remained healthy! Jake couldn't believe how brave he'd been and readily embraced opposite action from then on with his kids.

Parenting Exercise

Now it's your turn! Give the distress tolerance skills you learned in this chapter a shot over the coming days and weeks. As a reminder, here they are:

The CARE Skills

- Cool with ice, Activate your body, Relax your muscles, Exhale slowly

Opposite Action

- Do the exact opposite of what your unhelpful emotion urges are pulling for you to do.

Distraction

- Focus on something in the present moment other than the emotion or its components or do something that might generate an entirely different emotion.

Self-soothing

- Soothe yourself by focusing on comforting or pleasing sights, sounds, smells, tastes, or touches.

Mindfulness of Painful Thoughts and Feelings

- Notice painful thoughts or feelings without judging them or trying to change or hold onto them, redirecting your attention back to observing these inner experiences whenever your mind wanders elsewhere.

Although this list isn't especially long, it can be difficult to remember to use these skills when emotions are running high; thus, it may be helpful to put this list in strategic locations, just as Jake did. And as noted previously, practicing these skills when you aren't especially heated will likely make it easier to use them when you are on the verge of losing it. So, go ahead and test out these skills as often as you can while noticing how it feels to use them and what happens as a result. Do they help you refrain from acting on unwanted or unhelpful urges when with your kids? If so, keep using them! If not, keep using them anyway and try following them up with additional ART Tools to help you accept, regulate, and tolerate your emotions. The more you do so, the more likely it is that you'll one day be able to ride out even the most intense emotional storms without making things worse for you or your kids. I promise, it really is worth the effort.

Reference

Linehan, M. M. (2015). *DBT skills training manual* (2nd ed.). The Guilford Press.

Part 3

Applying the ART (<u>A</u>ccept, <u>R</u>egulate, <u>T</u>olerate) and Science of Emotions in Our Messy, Everyday Lives

When the Weather Is Sunny and Calm   **6**

Prioritize Connection Through Acceptance and Curiosity

Despite how hard parenting sometimes seems, it's rarely ever experienced as all doom and gloom. Yes, although parenting often feels daunting and overwhelming, there are also shining moments, even if only brief ones, when things just seem joyful and easy. You know, the small slivers in time when our kids seem eager to please and to be pleased. Or the handful of minutes or hours when our kids seem content playing on their own or even with each other. While it's easy to take these pockets of time for granted and to focus on troubleshooting the more trying moments of parenting instead, the choices that we make during these more peaceful times matter as well. Thus, in this chapter I discuss strategies for making the most of these calmer periods in order to bond more deeply with our children and potentially extend these windows of time. More specifically, I share one family's story to discuss how we can use the ART Tools to connect with our kids, as what comes intuitively to many of us doesn't necessarily serve us (or our kids) all that well in the long run. So, let's take a deep dive into different ways of connecting, starting with what many parents assume is required of them in order to foster strong relationships with their kids. Next, we'll move on to a more effective and much less emotionally draining approach to building loving, fulfilling, and secure bonds with our children.

DOI: 10.4324/9781003428343-10

Camilla's Story

I met Camilla, a devoted and expectant mom, when her then-only child, Evie, was three years old. At the time, Camilla was working long hours as a physician and strived to maximize the small pockets of time she had each day with Evie in an attempt to compensate for the many hours they spent apart from one another. As a result, Camilla tried hard to ensure that Evie was happy and having fun whenever they were together. To this end, Camilla often encouraged Evie to play with whatever she believed Evie would most enjoy, serving as the lead actor in their playtime together in order to keep Evie optimally entertained. For instance, Camilla regularly brought out new toys for Evie to play with, even when Evie was already happily playing with something else, and she frequently demonstrated for Evie how to best use each item. Camilla also talked loudly and animatedly as they played and excitedly announced whenever she had a new idea for what they might play next. Whether it was building a tower, dressing a doll, playing make-believe, or putting down train tracks, Camilla enthusiastically guided Evie's play, hoping to make it as magical and engaging as possible.

Not surprisingly, Evie seemed to thoroughly enjoy playtime with her mom and also basked in her mother's praise, which Camilla doled out generously. Whenever Evie followed instructions or figured out how to do something new, Camilla would clap and cheer, "Yay! Good girl!" and pull Evie in for a giant hug. And when Evie struggled with something and started to get frustrated or angry, Camilla would rush in to help resolve whatever difficulty Evie had encountered while reassuring her that there was "no need to cry" and that she was "okay." Sometimes Camilla even sang a silly song, offered a cookie, or tickled Evie in these moments in an attempt to distract her from whatever had been causing her so much distress. Camilla also proudly described herself as a "pushover parent" because she tended to refrain from setting and holding limits so as to avoid upsetting Evie.

As you might imagine, those in Camilla's orbit frequently commented on what a wonderful mom Camilla was. In their eyes, she was totally nailing this parenting thing. Yet, Camilla shared with me that she frequently felt completely drained by her time with Evie and worried that the life she had created for Evie wasn't sustainable, especially given that a new baby would soon be in the picture. Convinced that change was necessary but unsure how to bring it about, Camilla reached out for help. Over the course of several conversations, I gave Camilla five suggestions, each rooted in one or more of the ART Tools and/or principles from respectful parenting, and each applicable to varying degrees for parents of children of all ages. Here's what I recommended.

Suggestion 1: Stop Entertaining

I don't know about you, but just hearing about how hard Camilla was working to entertain Evie made me feel absolutely exhausted. And I wasn't even the one doing the work! Accordingly, the first tip I gave Camilla was to conserve her resources and stop trying to be Evie's entertainer in order to render her less vulnerable to painful emotions. I also pointed out that in addition to wearing herself out by taking on this role, Camilla was inadvertently interfering with Evie's self-directed play and motivation. Instead of Evie getting to decide what, how, and when to play with or stop playing with a given toy, Camilla was making these decisions for her, thus setting Evie up to continue being dependent on her to fill this role. Relatedly, by directing and overpraising Evie's play, Camilla was unwittingly encouraging Evie to look to others when deciding how to spend her time, as opposed to listening to her own intuitive wants, needs, and curiosities. Moreover, Evie was missing out on the benefits of independent play, which has been shown to predict better self-regulation (defined as the ability to plan, regulate emotions, and control impulses) years later in both toddlers and preschoolers (Colliver et al., 2022).

When I shared all of this with Camilla, her initial response was one of both surprise and relief. It had never occurred to Camilla that her toddler was fully capable of entertaining herself, and the thought of no longer taking on this responsibility was incredibly freeing. Camilla was even more surprised when I explained that the baby she was carrying would be able to do the same, beginning on day one. "What?!?!" she exclaimed. "There's no way a newborn baby can possibly entertain itself!" And chances are you may be thinking the very same thing right now. After all, our society tends to view and portray babies as cute, helpless blobs, rather than as the curious, tiny people they are from the very moment they arrive in this world.

Indeed, contrary to what many of us believe, babies are naturally wired to learn and explore and are much more easily stimulated or entertained than we may realize. Newborn babies inherently possess what mindfulness experts call "beginner's mind," meaning that they are able to observe and interact with the world without making the kinds of assumptions and judgments that most of us tend to make about how things should look. As a result, every moment of a newborn's life is filled with learning and play, even if these moments look dull and boring to us. The way the leaves rustle in the wind, the sounds of older children playing outside, the feel of the shaggy carpet touching their skin, and so on, are all moments of intrigue for even the youngest of babies. Hence, although babies require us to be nearby to care for their basic needs (feeding, changing, bathing, cuddling, etc.), as those in the respectful parenting world have noted, they do not need us to keep them occupied (Gerber, 2012; Lansbury, 2014). In fact, as is the case with older children, when we try to direct a baby's attention onto what we think might be interesting or fun, we run the risk of interfering with the very important, self-driven learning and play that they are already doing.

Like many parents I work with, Camilla was astonished by this information and she especially liked the idea of paving the way for the kind of relationship she'd like to have with her soon-to-arrive baby from the get-go. And for good reason: Changing the dynamic between her and Evie three years in proved to be easier said than done and required a great deal of patience.

Expecting that this shift would likely be difficult for both her and Evie, Camilla decided that she would start small, scaling back her role in Evie's playtime little by little. This kind of incremental change is what most cognitive-behavioral therapists recommend whenever making any kind of behavioral transformation. First, she committed to not bringing out new toys for Evie to play with if Evie was already in the middle of playing with something. To Camilla's surprise, when uninterrupted, Evie often played contentedly for many minutes with even the simplest of toys and household objects. Even items that seemed boring to Camilla, such as an empty shoebox, seemed to fascinate her daughter. And yet, it was when Evie was engrossed in exploring and manipulating these types of items that Camilla had the hardest time resisting the urge to bring out toys that *she* found to be more exciting.

Camilla also struggled initially to refrain from teaching Evie the "correct" way to use her toys. However, to her surprise, Evie didn't seem to mind when Camilla eventually started stepping back in this way. Although Camilla hadn't added a new toy to Evie's playroom in months, Evie played with the toys that were in there as though she'd never seen them before. She transformed wooden blocks into food for her dolls, turned nesting cups into targets that she tried to hit with a bouncy ball, and used the wooden food in her pretend sushi bar as money for the car wash that she made out of magnetic tiles.

After a few weeks, Camilla decided to take even more of a backseat during Evie's playtime, particularly when drawing and during Evie's "make-believe" play. This is where things got rocky. Since she could mostly only scribble, Evie had gotten used to her mom drawing whatever she asked her to draw. She had also grown accustomed to Camilla creating and directing imaginative scenes for them to act out of pirates searching for treasure, princesses getting ready for balls, and doctors caring for babies. Understandably, Evie did not like Camilla pulling back here one bit and made her displeasure known through epic tantrums and unkind, angry words that she lobbed at her mom each time Camilla declined to orchestrate these creative pursuits.

Over time, Evie's outbursts lessened, and she began to appear more comfortable drawing on her own and creating her own imaginary worlds. However, this transformation did not occur overnight and required Camilla to sit with some pretty challenging emotions and behaviors while continuing to hold firm limits around what she was and wasn't willing to do. I'll elaborate on what this kind of limit setting involved shortly, but for now, I'll just note that Camilla would likely still be drawing for Evie and directing Evie's pretend play had she not been willing to face the music of Evie's distress and the discomfort that this stirred up in herself. In other words, aside from giving in to Evie's demands (which Camilla was determined to stop doing), there wasn't a way to stem or circumvent Evie's anger.

It's also worth noting here that one of the things that helped Camilla weather Evie's storms in these moments was knowing that kids are, generally speaking, highly adaptable. Sure, they may protest change at times, but once they understand that what they're fighting isn't up for debate, they tend to adjust fairly quickly. And that's exactly what happened with Evie. In fact, Evie not only now draws and engages in make-believe play on her own (sometimes with Camilla joining in parallel or as a supporting character), but she actually seems to prefer this kind of creative, independent play. She loves when Camilla watches her or mindfully participates in what she's doing, but she doesn't need Camilla to play *for* her anymore and sometimes even chooses to play where Camilla isn't, clearly enjoying her time alone to act out the fantastical worlds that she has dreamed up all by herself.

Plus, according to Camilla, a bonus perk is that she now has more time to do the things she needs and wants to do. Whether it's cleaning the house, reading a book, making dinner, or changing her newborn's diaper, Camilla has much more time on her hands these days and feels much less frazzled and vulnerable as a result, even with an infant now in the mix.

But how, you ask, does a parent of a daredevil or Little Miss Mess let their kids play without supervision? The key is to set our kids up for success by creating what respectful parenting expert Janet Lansbury calls a "yes space" where your child can safely play without interruption from you (Lansbury, 2021). Whether big or small, this space simply needs to be free of child hazards and contain only safe, age-appropriate toys that can be played with however your child likes without risking damage to themselves, your house, or your property. In other words, you might want to keep your new white couch and your grandmother's crystal out of this space. Similarly, depending on your child's age, scissors and permanent markers might be best kept elsewhere as well.

It's also worth mentioning that if you have kids of different ages, you may need more than one of these spaces. This may be the case even if you have kids who are close in age. For instance, your five-year-old may need a space where he can build with those tiny Legos you keep stepping on without having to worry about his little brother destroying his creation or choking on the head of a decapitated Lego dude. By the same token, if your six- and eight-year-olds are fighting like cats and dogs more days than not, they may need separate play spaces as well, even if they both generally like to play with the same few toys. Obviously, creating distinct play areas for each of your kids can be tricky, especially if you live in a small space or have many kids. That said, as noted previously, these spaces need not be large. Section off part of a hallway or a small corner of a room with a baby gate, drop in a few developmentally desirable toys, childproof whatever needs childproofing, and voila, you're set!

Of course, if your kids aren't used to playing on their own, it might take some time for them to adjust to this. Let them know that the space is theirs and begin by spending time with them in it. Fill the area with some of their favorite toys, as well as some new ones they haven't seen yet. Then, after you've mindfully spent some time together there, let your child know that you will be stepping away for a bit to wash dishes, do some laundry, or make a phone call, and then check in with them a few minutes later, gradually increasing the time spent away over the next few days, weeks, or even months.

Naturally, as your kids age, these customized play areas will likely become a thing of the past. However, this tip of not entertaining applies for parents of older kids and teens as well, not just toddlers. After all, although how we go about entertaining older children might look different, it's easy to feel pulled to try to entertain our kids when they're bored, no matter their ages. To be clear, if you're up for playing Monopoly with your ten-year-old, going to the mall with your teenager, or taking your tween on a hike, go for it! However, please know that it's also okay to let your older kids be bored for an hour – or even most of the day – while you rest or get stuff done. After all, boredom breeds creativity, so giving your kids time to fill on their own will likely prove beneficial to them as well. In fact, a number of studies have shown positive, immediate, and long-term effects of independent activity (including unstructured, free play) on mental well-being in children of all ages; and it is believed that a decline in such activity over the past few decades may be a primary cause of the well-documented, co-occurring decline in youth mental health (Gray et al., 2023). Having said that, if your kids are used to spending every spare minute of their downtime doing activities with you, you may need to gradually scale this back, in much the same way that Camilla did with Evie.

Suggestion 2: Mindfully Notice

One of Camilla's concerns when we first discussed her ceasing to play the role of Evie's entertainer was that their bond might weaken as a result. I, however, was confident that, if anything, their connection would only grow stronger with this change. The reason? At the same time that I encouraged Camilla to stop entertaining Evie, I also suggested that she spend more time mindfully noticing her daughter, knowing that this mindful observation would not only help her better understand and appreciate Evie and the way her brain works, but that it would also help Evie feel more seen and known by the most important person in her world. Once again, this suggestion is one I make to parents of older kids and teens as well.

After explaining what mindfulness is and the benefits of it (see Chapter 3 for a refresher), Camilla and I began to discuss the ways in which she might practice mindfulness in order to deepen her connection with Evie. Given that Camilla was most troubled when thinking about the potential impact of changing her approach to playtime, this is where we initially focused.

Since Evie was used to her mom's near-constant presence and entertainment when Camilla wasn't at work, I suggested that Camilla begin by spending the same amount of time with Evie that she used to when at home, with only some of this time being devoted to mindfully noticing Evie. As noted in Chapter 3, round-the-clock mindfulness practice isn't realistic for most of us, so I knew that any more than a few minutes at a time of mindful observation would likely set Camilla up for failure. Thus, to begin, I suggested Camilla aim for 5–10 minutes per day of mindful observation during Evie's playtime and reminded her to simply redirect her attention back onto Evie's play whenever her mind wandered elsewhere.

How she spent the rest of Evie's playtime really depended on her mood, as well as Evie's. On some days, after her 5–10 minutes of practice were up, Camilla watched Evie play in a less mindful way, allowing herself to daydream or think about her list of things to do. On other days, she laid on the couch and informed Evie that she was going to catch up on her reading, the news, email, etc., while Evie played next to her. Then there were the days when she popped in headphones and let Evie know that she'd be right by her side listening to music or a podcast. Eventually, she began spending this time apart from Evie, leaving Evie to play contentedly on her own while she worked or hung out in other areas of the house.

Although Camilla enjoyed these breaks from having to be "on," she also relished her mindful observation time and found that it enabled her to appreciate Evie in an entirely new way; discovering, for instance, that her daughter was much more creative, thoughtful, and industrious than she had ever realized. Accordingly, Camilla began to carve out more 5–10 minute increments for this practice throughout the day, which not only helped her feel closer to Evie, but also gave way to an increase in the amount of time that Evie seemed to feel comfortable with Camilla stepping away. It was almost as if these brief moments of mindful noticing filled Evie's cup, satiating her need for connection and giving way to longer and longer stretches of time during which she seemed content playing without Camilla.

Over time, Camilla also began to bring mindful noticing to the caregiving aspects of her time with Evie, including mealtime, bathtime, and bedtime. Once again, Camilla reported being amazed at just how competent her toddler naturally was. Prior to learning about mindfulness, Camilla had taken charge of each of these pockets of time with Evie. At meals, she tried to hold Evie's attention with silly stories or games in hopes of keeping Evie eating and at the table. Similarly, during bathtime, Camilla put on elaborate shows with Evie's bath toys and washed Evie's hair and body for her. And at bedtime, Camilla picked out and put Evie's pajamas on her, brushed Evie's hair and teeth, and selected a book for them to read together.

Things changed drastically when Camilla began swapping out *doing for* Evie with mindful observation, as she discovered that Evie didn't need much of the entertainment or help that she'd been providing. To Camilla's surprise, Evie happily ate her meals without distraction, getting up when her belly was full, but typically not beforehand. She beamed as her mom sat on the edge of the tub while she proudly washed her own body and hair with only minimal assistance from Camilla, and she excitedly picked out her bedtime books and pajamas and changed all by herself when given the opportunity to do so. Of course, Camilla still helped Evie at times, but she generally found that she was able to do much less and delight significantly more during these caregiving moments thanks to this new, more mindful approach that she'd adopted.

Having said that, it's worth noting that not every child will roll with such a significant shift so smoothly. Meals may not be fully eaten for a stretch and tantrums may ensue demanding a return to the way things once were. We'll talk about how to navigate tantrums and other challenging behaviors in Chapter 7, but for now, just remember that kids are highly adaptable, even if they initially protest change. In other words, my recommendation to mindfully notice more (and otherwise do less) would still stand, no matter how your kids feel about this.

Naturally, what you choose to mindfully notice when caring for babies and older children will likely look different from the activities Camilla chose for her practice when with Evie. For example, when Camilla's baby was born, she mindfully observed her baby girl do things like nurse, lay in her crib after waking from a nap, and try to roll from her belly to her back – all of which she had either interrupted or missed as opportunities to observe when Evie was a baby.

Even as your kids grow and your caregiving role becomes a fraction of what it once was, you can still take advantage of whatever moments arise to practice mindful observation. For instance, you may choose to mindfully observe your tween shoot hoops in the backyard or draw at his desk. Or, maybe you mindfully observe your teenager put on makeup for the prom or celebrate with her teammates after a big win. Or, if your kids are in a phase where they seem to want to have nothing to do with you, maybe you steal whatever moments you can get to practice. For example, you may simply mindfully notice your kids' facial and body expressions as they pile into the car at school pickup or as they slump on the couch at the end of a long day. Even these brief bits of mindful noticing can go a long way toward helping you understand your kids and what's going on for them in the moment, thus potentially better enabling you to meet them where they're at and connect in ways that will work for both of you.

Suggestion 3: Mindfully Participate

To some, parents who take a mindful approach to parenting, such as that just described, may look lazy, detached, or disengaged. In all honesty, that likely would have been my impression when I first started my parenting journey. However, I have since learned that nothing could be further from the truth. In fact, as Camilla discovered, mindful observation is an intentional, effortful endeavor that helps us be much more present, engaged, and attuned with our kids than when we are on autopilot, doing things for them that we assume they require without really taking time to notice what they're actually needing. Plus, mindful noticing helps us better read the room so that we can pivot to mindful participation when that's needed, desired, or both.

Crucially, as I explained to Camilla, mindful parenting is *not* about checking out and letting our kids raise themselves. Rather, it's about tuning in to see our kids as they are in a given moment and responding contingently to what they're telling us, both verbally and non-verbally. Thus, Camilla's mindful observation practice helped her better discern when to participate mindfully, when to simply sit back and continue watching Evie, and when to shift to doing something entirely for herself. And as was the case with mindful observation, Camilla found that playtime and caregiving tasks both lent themselves nicely to mindful participation.

Although playing with Evie had always come fairly naturally to Camilla, she had to make some minor adjustments when mindfully participating in Evie's play. As mentioned previously, Camilla was used to taking the lead in her playtime with Evie, and she soon found that playtime was less enjoyable – and sometimes even boring – when she wasn't calling the shots. As a result, she had to work hard when participating mindfully to notice and resist giving in to urges to either resume her role as the director of play or check out entirely. We therefore discussed practicing in short increments of time to start and doing so with activities that she found inherently fun, such as playing soccer and having tea parties with Evie.

Outside of playtime, Camilla found it much easier to practice mindful participation. Whether brushing Evie's teeth, singing songs with Evie on the way to daycare, or baking with Evie, Camilla was able to focus fully on the given activity, just as she always had. Although this became somewhat more challenging once Evie's sister was born, giving her newborn time to play on her own – something she'd never done when Evie was a baby – made it easier to continue this practice with only occasional interruptions.

Likewise, Evie's independent playtime also made it easier for Camilla to participate mindfully when with her baby, Anya. Instead of having a toddler tugging at her shirt and begging her to play while she changed Anya's diapers or bathed her, Camilla was able to mostly focus completely on these caregiving tasks. And, at my prompting, she did so mindfully while narrating or describing for Anya what she was doing each step of the way, so that her baby could gradually begin to participate as well. For example, while changing Anya's diapers, she would say something along the lines of the following: "I'm going to lay you down here on the changing table so I can put a new diaper on you. And now let's take off your pants . . . and unfasten your diaper . . . and lift your legs a bit so I can clean you off with this wipe. And now let's wipe a few times . . . put on some Butt Paste . . . and slide a new diaper in there. Alright, almost done. We just have to fasten that diaper . . . and pull up those pants. And that's it! We're all done so I'm going to pick you back up again."

Although Camilla thought it seemed silly at first when I suggested she narrate in this way for Anya, after a few weeks of doing so, she told me that it not only helped her participate more mindfully, but that it also seemed, to her amazement, to allow Anya to do so as well. When she was only a few months old, Anya started lifting her legs up for Camilla during diaper changes, almost as though she understood Camilla's words as to what was about to happen next. Of course, as our kids get older, there's no need to narrate every step of these caregiving moments. For instance, I mostly brush my son's teeth in silence as he knows exactly what to expect during these two minutes. However, for babies, everything is new, so describing what we're doing in words likely helps them begin to understand their world, as well as the words we're using. Indeed, research suggests that infants as young as six months demonstrate understanding of commonly spoken words (Bergelson & Swingley, 2012), suggesting that they comprehend more than we might expect.

Again, with older kids and teens, mindful participation is likely going to look very different, even though the same guiding principles still apply. Whatever you are doing together, the key is that you participate fully, without judgment and without distraction. So, if you are playing catch outside with your 12-year-old, then just play catch, without daydreaming or judging your kid for the balls he drops. Or better said, if and when you inevitably notice your mind wandering to these or other thoughts, gently bring yourself back to mindfully playing catch, as many times as needed. And if you're reuniting after a day apart, give your full attention to your kids and actively listen to what they share, following up with non-judgmental reflections and questions to learn more and better understand their experiences.

Suggestion 4: Set and Hold Firm Limits

As noted previously, Camilla proudly described herself as a pushover parent, believing that it was better to let Evie do or have what she wanted than to set a limit that would upset her. After all, why say no to a second, third, or even fourth cookie if doing so would leave Evie in tears? At the same time, Camilla sometimes felt uncomfortable giving in to Evie's demands.

For example, she didn't love the idea of letting Evie overwater their lawn, but she allowed her to do so anyway because Evie would resist whenever she was told it was time to turn off the water. She also didn't love letting Evie come into her bed at night – largely because she didn't sleep well with Evie rolling around next to her – and yet she decided that this was preferable to having to deal with a full-blown tantrum while half asleep. In addition, sometimes Camilla had to set limits for safety reasons, but even then, she felt uneasy doing so and would get flustered by the meltdowns that would ensue.

Thus, although Camilla believed that her permissive parenting style worked well at times, she recognized that it might not be the most useful long-term strategy and that it was likely contributing to her feeling exhausted and overwhelmed, thus leaving her more vulnerable to other painful emotions. Indeed, she acknowledged that she sometimes found herself getting annoyed or angry with Evie for doing some of the things she allowed Evie to do.

And of course she was! We've all likely been there before. Our kid says no to our instructions or requests, so we retract whatever we said in order to avoid an emotional outburst, even though we're feeling pretty irritated that they're not just cooperating. Meanwhile, the more we walk on eggshells around our kids, the more frazzled and less in control we feel. Plus, as I've personally discovered time and again, when we abandon the limits we've set in order to avoid upsetting our kids, we sometimes wind up with a big mess on our hands, rattling us even further and making it harder to show up as we'd like.

To be clear, I'm not saying that you should always hold a limit you've set. On the contrary, sometimes we reflexively set unreasonable limits that we later realize aren't needed or helpful. However, it's important to be honest with ourselves as to why we are retracting a limit when we make the choice to do so. If our decision stems from recognizing that the limit is truly unnecessary or impractical, then so be it – out the window it can go! Yet, if the choice to backpedal is driven by our desire to people-please and avoid upsetting our kids, then it might be worth holding the limit and welcoming whatever storm happens to follow.

In light of this, one of the tips I gave Camilla was to practice setting and holding limits that were needed for safety, well-being, and/or sanity-preserving (i.e., reducing emotional vulnerability) purposes, no matter Evie's response. And since Evie's bedsharing habits were disrupting Camilla's sleep, thus contributing to her feeling exhausted and overwhelmed, I strongly suggested she start there. Specifically, I recommended that Camilla take time out of the day, well before bedtime, to inform Evie that in order to help both of them get the best night's sleep possible, they would each be sleeping in their own beds moving forward.

As you might imagine, Camilla initially laughed at this suggestion and said that Evie would surely venture over to her bed at some point in the night, even if she agreed ahead of time that she would stop doing so. And of course, I knew that Camilla would likely be right. In fact, I told Camilla that I would be shocked if Evie *didn't* try climbing back into her bed. However, I also reminded Camilla that her job would not only be to set this limit but to actually enforce it as well. Thus, we discussed letting Evie know that if she tried to come into her mom's bed, Camilla would walk her back to her own room as Camilla was a light sleeper and always woke up whenever Evie came in at night.

Unsurprisingly, Evie was not a fan of this plan. Although she didn't seem especially distressed when Camilla presented these new expectations first thing in the morning, by bedtime, it was a whole different story. Evie usually went to bed fairly easily on her own (it was just in the middle of the night that she wandered over to Camilla's bed), but on this night, she seemed determined not to sleep and begged Camilla to read her one more story, get her one last glass of water, answer one last question, give her one more hug, and so on. Camilla lovingly but firmly agreed to acquiesce once, and only once, to each of these requests and then reminded Evie what would happen that night.

Around 11 pm, Evie woke up and came into Camilla's room. As she started climbing up onto Camilla's bed, Camilla awoke and said, "Oops, sorry sweetie, I can't let you sleep in here tonight. I'll walk you to your room though and help you get back into your bed." As Camilla predicted, Evie did not like this at all and started crying and begging Camilla to let her stay. Thankfully, we'd discussed ahead of time what to do should Evie have this kind of reaction. First, Camilla calmly acknowledged and validated Evie's distress at the change by saying, "You really want to sleep in my bed tonight like you used to and are upset that I'm not letting you. It's hard having to sleep in your own bed." Next, she conveyed confidence in Evie by adding, "I know you can do it," while holding Evie's hand and walking her back to her room. Finally, she tucked Evie in, gave her a big hug, and promised that they could cuddle together in the morning. Although they went through a similar process two more times later that same night (and a few more times over the next few nights), Evie ended up sleeping in her bed the entire night and every night thereafter and now rarely ever comes into Camilla's room at night.

Building on this success, Camilla began to set and hold other limits in a similar fashion, welcoming whatever emotions these evoked in Evie (or herself) while maintaining the boundaries she'd set. With practice, Camilla became increasingly comfortable setting and holding limits that were important for Evie's safety or well-being, such as insisting on holding Evie's hand in parking lots and not snacking on anything other than veggies right before dinner. She found it a little trickier, however, to resist her urges to cave when setting limits for the sake of her own comfort or convenience, such as not letting Evie start messy art projects right before company was to arrive and not letting Evie play with her carefully styled hair. As a result, this was touch and go at first, with Camilla sometimes giving in or backing down at the very first sign of distress or bribing Evie to comply. Interestingly, however, the more confident Camilla grew in her ability to hold even these limits, the more at ease Evie seemed to be and the less she protested the limits that Camilla did set. In fact, she almost seemed to take comfort in knowing that Camilla meant what she said and was no longer willing to look the other way or bend over backwards to accommodate Evie's every desire. Much like bowling with bumpers, Evie could now count on Camilla to stop her from doing things she wasn't supposed to do, which freed her to roll as she pleased in the interim.

And yes, the same goes for older kids, tweens, and teens. Whether setting limits around screen time, curfew, school attendance, clothing, substance use, or whatever, we can allow our kids to bump up against these limits without bending them, even if explosions ensue. That said, as noted earlier, there may be times where we make the conscious choice to withdraw a previously set limit. For instance, although my husband and I initially set a firm, no-bikini limit for our tween daughter, we decided to let this go after we learned that all of the girls in her grade had purchased matching, age-appropriate bikinis to wear on their school's water park day. Had we not given in, our daughter would have been the only odd girl out, which didn't seem fair to her. That said, we continue to hold our no-smartphone limit and intend to do so until after eighth grade, if not later, despite our daughter's pleas for one as more and more of her friends get these devices.[1]

---

1 As an aside, if you haven't checked out waituntil8th.org, I highly encourage you to do so. It's packed with research and information on why it's worth waiting to give smartphones to kids until at least age 14. Plus, they've organized a pledge that you can sign, promising not to give your kid a smartphone until at least the end of eighth grade, assuming 10 or more other families from your child's grade and school also sign the pledge.

Suggestion 5: Welcome All Emotions

It goes without saying that all moments of calm will inevitably come to an end, no matter how "easy" your kids happen to be. While some kids may have more outbursts than others, all children will at one point or another express – in some shape or form – frustration, anger, anxiety, disappointment, jealousy, etc. Although I'll dive much more into how to navigate the blowups that our kids sometimes have in the next chapter, whether in response to limits we've set or not, I want to briefly touch on this here given that even the calmest of days will likely contain at least a few emotional hiccups.

As it happens, the final and perhaps most important tip I gave Camilla was to welcome all of Evie's emotions, and eventually those of her soon-to-arrive baby, rather than try to fix or shut down these feelings in some way. If you remember, prior to our conversations, Camilla believed it was her job to keep Evie happy at all times and strived to soothe, reassure, or distract away any painful emotions that Evie experienced. In fact, like many parents, Camilla had sung "Hush Little Baby" whenever Evie cried as an infant and, as Evie grew, she continued to pacify any distress with variations of "aww, don't cry" or "it's okay." And when these well-intentioned sayings failed to do the trick, Camilla would bring out treats or a playful game in hopes of distracting Evie out of her feelings.

As Camilla acknowledged, however, being the keeper and lifter of Evie's spirits was tiring and sometimes even frustrating. Plus, as I explained to Camilla and have written about previously (Jerud, 2019), there's almost always a reason for children's tears, as well as their outbursts. Indeed, crying is one of the few tools that infants and young children have to communicate their needs to us – a diaper that requires changing, eyes that want to sleep, or a tummy that's hungry for food. Even when these basic needs have been met, crying and acting out both sometimes function as ways for kids (and teens) to release pent-up feelings from moments or even days prior. Thus, seemingly dramatic reactions to otherwise trivial events often have little to do with the events that just transpired. Instead, these intense responses can be seen as indicators that our kid is struggling and needs our help. Permission to feel is, many times, all that's needed.

Unfortunately, when we shush a howling baby or say "you're okay" to an intensely distraught toddler, we inadvertently invalidate our kid's experience and convey the message that we don't want to hear what he or she is trying to communicate to us. It's as though our child is saying, "No! I don't like this!" and we are responding by saying, "Yes, yes, you do."

Similarly, when we coax our kids to share when they don't want to share, bribe them to do things they don't want to do, or force an apology they aren't yet ready to give, we again communicate to them that their wishes aren't important to us and that they should stifle their emotions in order to appease others. Regrettably, rather than help our kids become the well-adjusted, empathic individuals that most of us hope they will grow up to be, these types of responses teach them that what they feel is irrelevant or even wrong and may also leave them thinking that those who are in positions of power are allowed to control vulnerable, less powerful individuals. What's more, when we try to avoid or dismiss our kids' feelings in these ways, we often end up working much harder than we need to while missing out on the incredible bonding that can occur when we take the time to see the world through our kids' eyes.

With this in mind, Camilla and I discussed welcoming all of Evie's feelings, rather than trying to brush these aside or make her feel better. For instance, if Evie were to become frustrated when playing with a toy, Camilla's job would simply be to acknowledge (not fix) what she was seeing. She might say something along the lines of, "Ugh, you're so frustrated! It's not working like you want it to," and provide assistance if, and only if, asked. Even then, I suggested helping minimally, such as by wondering aloud as to what might happen if a piece was moved to another spot. Again, I stressed that the goal would not be to get rid of Evie's frustration, but instead to help Evie learn that she can tolerate feeling frustrated without having to give up or rely on Camilla to help her escape what she's feeling.

Likewise, we discussed allowing Evie to cry and whine on her own terms, without trying to put an end to either. In other words, rather than try to turn Evie's cries into giggles or convince her that there's no need to get so upset, I suggested that Camilla welcome and acknowledge the emotions behind Evie's tears and complaints.

For example, Evie did not like her parents going out for date nights and would almost always cry and protest in the minutes leading up to their departure. In the past, Camilla and her husband, Andre, would tell Evie there was no need to cry because she would have so much fun with her grandma while they were out; plus, they'd only be gone for a few hours. Although both were true, Evie tended to respond to these statements by crying even louder and grabbing onto her parents' legs in an effort to get them to stay. Her parents, in turn, would then resort to tickling Evie in hopes of getting her to let go – both literally and figuratively. Unfortunately, this, too, only seemed to make Evie more upset.

Interestingly, however, the moment Camilla and Andre shifted to acknowledging and validating Evie's sadness, everything changed. Prior to heading out for their next date night, they told Evie that it made sense she was sad because she didn't want them to leave. To their surprise, Evie nodded her head, hugged them both, and ran off to play with her grandma.

It turned out that all Evie ever really needed on date nights was to know that her parents understood and accepted how she felt. Feeling seen, she no longer felt the need to fight for their acceptance and could instead move through her sadness and on to other things. However, even if Evie's distress had intensified in response to this new approach, I still would have recommended welcoming her feelings in full.

After all, this kind of acceptance is what generally enables all of us – both kids and adults – to ride the waves of the painful emotions that show up within us, without getting swept away by them. Thus, whether your eight-year-old is complaining that he hates his lunch, your 11-year-old is jealous that his sister got an award when he didn't, or your 16-year-old is fuming because you won't buy her a new phone, welcoming these feelings and allowing them to run their natural course can be incredibly freeing – not only for us but also for our kids.

Parenting Exercise

Once again, now it's your turn. No matter your children's ages, give each of the suggestions listed in this chapter a try over the next few days, weeks, and months. For quick reference, here they are:

1) Stop entertaining
   - Let your kids decide what to play with and how they are going to do so without interfering. Resist any urges to play *for* your kids or to teach them how a certain toy works.
2) Mindfully notice
   - Mindfully notice your children for a few minutes at a time as they play and during basic caregiving tasks, redirecting your attention back onto your children whenever your mind wanders elsewhere.
3) Mindfully participate
   - Fully engage in play with your kids without checking out or directing how the play unfolds. During caregiving tasks, focus entirely on the activity at hand, without distraction. If you do become distracted, gently shift your attention back to participating mindfully.
4) Set and hold firm limits
   - Calmly set and hold limits that are needed for safety, well-being, and/or sanity-preserving purposes, even if your kids loudly protest these limits.

5) Welcome all emotions
    - Accept your children's emotions in full and allow them to feel intense, uncomfortable emotions without trying to fix or avoid these feelings.

As a reminder, your kids need not approve of these changes in order for you to make them. Stay the course, whenever possible, knowing that the more you follow these suggestions, the more comfortable you and your kids will likely become with these new ways of interacting. Also, keep in mind that it's okay to take whatever pace feels right for you, even if that means only implementing one of these suggestions at a time. As is always the case when trying to change behavior, even small movements in the right direction are better than none.

References

Bergelson, E. & Swingley, D. (2012). At 6-9 months, human infants know the meanings of many common nouns. *Psychological and Cognitive Sciences, 109*(9), 3253–3258. https://www.pnas.org/doi/full/10.1073/pnas.1113380109

Colliver, Y., Harrison, L. J., Brown, J. E., & Humburg, P. (2022). Free play predicts self-regulation years later: Longitudinal evidence from a large Australian sample of toddlers and preschoolers. *Early Childhood Research Quarterly*, *59*, 148–161. https://doi.org/10.1016/j.ecresq.2021.11.011

Gerber, M. (2012). *Your self-confident baby: How to encourage your child's natural abilities – from the very start*. Trader Paper Press.

Gray, P., Lancy, D. F., & Bjorklund, D. F. (2023). Decline in independent activity as a cause of decline in children's mental well-being: Summary of the evidence. *The Journal of Pediatrics*, *260*, 113352. https://doi.org/10.1016/j.jpeds.2023.02.004

Jerud, A. (2019, December 4). *A novel strategy for preventing sexual violence? Treat kids with respect* [Blog post]. https://www.psychologytoday.com/us/blog/the-art-and -science-of-emotions/201912/a-novel-strategy-for-preventing-sexual-violence

Lansbury, J. (2014). *Elevating child care: A guide to respectful parenting*. CreateSpace Publishing.

Lansbury, J. (2021, June 23). *YES spaces – what they really are and why they matter* [Blog post]. https:// www.janetlansbury.com/2021/06/yes-spaces-what-they-really-are-and -why-they-matter/

When the Weather Is Stormy and Treacherous

7

Accept, Respond Contingently, and Move Strategically Until the Storm Passes

Although you likely now have some ideas as to how to more skillfully navigate the emotional storms that blow through your home, you may find yourself doubting whether you'll actually be able to successfully implement these strategies in the midst of extreme emotions. So, let's dive into the nitty-gritty of what to do when you're caught off guard and overwhelmed by the feelings raging within or outside of you. How, exactly, do you go about welcoming feelings when emotional storms are threatening to ruin the day? In the pages that follow, you'll find a collection of ART-informed pointers for moments when your kids, you, or all involved are emotionally flooded, as well as real-life parenting examples to give you a better sense of how to use the ART (Accept, Regulate, and Tolerate) Tools to help you survive these storms.

But first, it's worth noting that while emotionally charged days may be rare for some, for many of us, the conditions we face as parents are often (if not almost always) challenging. On some days, it's our kids who wake up on the wrong side of the bed. Their volume dial seems to be set to screaming-only mode, and they respond to every little thing that happens or doesn't happen as though it's a travesty. We may get yelled at, hit, kicked, or told that we are the "worst parent ever" just for breathing. On other days, we are the ones who make the day unpleasant. These tend to be the days when we are even more sleep deprived than usual, when we are in the midst

DOI: 10.4324/9781003428343-11

of an argument with our partner, when we have impossible deadlines to meet at work, when the sink is full of dirty, day-old dishes, when we didn't get a chance to drink our morning coffee, or when some version of all of the above (or worse) occurs. As a result, we show up impatient and cranky with our kids and wish that we could take a break from parenting for just a few minutes, hours, days, or even weeks. And then there are the days when everyone in the family is dysregulated, including us.

Fortunately, the skills needed for getting through emotional storms are similar regardless of a given storm's origins. What's more, you've actually learned these skills (the ART Tools) already in the previous chapters. And yet, because our kids' emotional displays often look and feel very different from our own, in this chapter I'll discuss our responses to each of these separately. First, I'll cover how to navigate our kids' emotional outbursts, since it's these that so often trigger our own. From there, I'll talk about how to get through days when we're on the verge of getting swept away by our *own* emotions. Finally, I'll go over what to do when our kids' storms are threatening to collide with our own, potentially giving way to the most treacherous conditions of all.

Critically, though we may not ever enjoy any of these storms, if we can accept them and see them as opportunities to teach our kids (and ourselves) that it's possible to sit with seemingly intolerable levels of distress without hurting those we love, then these moments can take on a new light. Rather than try to avoid these moments at all costs, we can embrace them when they arrive and capitalize on the valuable learning experiences they afford. After all, being able to weather powerful emotions requires not only skill but also practice. Thankfully, each time we find a way to slow down and move strategically through heated interactions, we become more adept at accepting, regulating, and tolerating overwhelming emotions. And who knows, with enough modeling and practice, one day – likely many moons in the future – so might our kids.

Responding to Our Kids' Emotional Storms

Although our kids' emotional storms are, in many ways, very similar to our own, their emotional outbursts often appear more intense, more frequent, and more perplexing (at least from our perspective) than ours. Indeed, as noted previously, the out-of-proportion reactions that kids of all ages have at times often have little to do with any one, identifiable prompting event, but instead function as much-needed, healthy releases for the many feelings they've been harboring for one reason or another. Given this, let's dive into some ART-informed do's and don'ts for responding to our children's challenging emotions more generally before moving on to specific considerations to keep in mind during the most common behavioral manifestations of these feelings. Specifically, we'll tackle – in the order that follows – how to navigate crying and whining, tantrums (yes, even older kids and teens have these), shouting and hurtful words, and dangerous or destructive behaviors. That said, if you're short on time, please feel free to jump ahead to the issue that you're currently struggling with the most.

General Suggestions

The common theme underlying each of the five suggestions that follow is acceptance. As a reminder, acceptance isn't about liking or approving the situation, nor is it about being a passive pushover. On the contrary, it's about looking into the eye of the storm and acknowledging the reality of the moment – exactly as it is – as opposed to insisting that things should be different in some way.

With this in mind, acceptance is what we want to strive for no matter the intensity or duration of our children's emotional explosions. After all, when it comes to feelings, there's no such thing as ones that are "too much" or "bad." And in many ways, our children's ages are somewhat irrelevant here as their brains aren't yet wired to reliably inhibit the urges that accompany powerful feelings (and won't be until their executive centers fully develop, around age 25; Casey et al., 2008). Thus, we don't have to give much weight to concerns about whether our kids are "too old" to act however they do when emotionally dysregulated. Or to put it another way, we can take comfort in knowing that seemingly age-inappropriate behaviors are actually quite appropriate when our children's immature executive centers have been emotionally hijacked. Having said that, you are the expert on your children and your family, so if you have concerns about any of your kids' behaviors, I recommend discussing these with a professional.

Suggestion 1: Once Again, Welcome the Storm

It likely goes without saying that our children's emotional outbursts are never fun to watch and can even be painful or frustrating for us to witness. On some occasions, the immense love we feel for our little ones can make it difficult to see them struggle or suffer and can leave us feeling as though our hearts have cracked open alongside theirs. Then there are the times where our children's meltdowns seem so ridiculous, inconvenient, or embarrassing that it's hard to empathize or convey anything other than anger, frustration, impatience, or annoyance.

Whether feeling heartbroken or fed up with our children's emotional outbursts, the pull that we *all* feel at times to try to quiet these – rather than welcome them in full – is completely natural and understandable. That said, when we give in to these urges to resist or hasten along our children's emotional storms, we (intentionally or unintentionally) send the message that we're not really okay with such outward expressions. In response, our kids may conclude that they shouldn't be feeling what they're feeling, at least not so intensely, or that we don't believe they're capable of tolerating powerful emotions. Of course, none of this is what we want and will likely make life harder for us and our kids in the long run, and possibly even in the short run as well.

Indeed, when we push back against our kids' emotions, it's as though we're trying to keep away the rain by holding buckets up to the sky in the middle of a downpour. Sure, we may be able to prevent some rain from hitting the ground for a bit, but it won't be long before the rain spills over the buckets and out onto the earth, leaving us feeling unnecessarily exhausted and defeated. Correspondingly, when we try to keep our kids' emotional storms at bay, we're likely to find ourselves feeling every bit as depleted. Thus, whether faced with a torrent of rain or our kids' emotional explosions, we might as well embrace the weather and let the storm descend as it may, rather than waste our time and energy trying to interfere.

In practice, this means holding back any judgments that we might have about our kids, not only for feeling the way they do, but also for how they choose to express these feelings. Obviously, this isn't easy and most of us *will* judge our kids in these ways from time to time. Yet, even if your kid is splayed out on the floor crying because you cut his peanut butter and jelly sandwich into triangles, not squares, I encourage allowing these tears without invalidating or trivializing them in any way. In that moment, your son is upset and has a right to be however upset he happens to be for however long he happens to be upset. There's no need to try to convince him otherwise, nor is there a need to appease him by making a new, squared sandwich. There's also no need to drop everything or cancel your plans because of his squalls. Just as you would still head to work or a birthday party in a rainstorm, you can carry on eating breakfast, packing your bag, or doing whatever else it is you were doing before the blowup. Or, if you have the time, patience, and energy to do so, you can sit near your child as he wails. Whatever you do, the key is simply to welcome the outburst – in word, tone, and demeanor – knowing that just like any other storm, it, too, will eventually pass.

Yes, I realize it might seem bizarre to respond to such an over-the-top reaction as though it is anything but aggravating and unnecessary. And yet, imagine for a minute if your partner, friend, or even therapist responded to one of your own meltdowns about something seemingly inconsequential as though it were a sign that you were immature and overly sensitive. It wouldn't feel so good, right? Their response might even leave you feeling more upset.

With this in mind, whenever judgmental thoughts about your kids' emotional displays arise, see if you can notice these thoughts (without latching onto them or treating them as facts) and then gently shift your attention onto mindfully observing the moment. Relatedly, keep in mind that comparisons between your child and others will almost invariably give way to unhelpful judgments, so it's worth redirecting your attention away from these as well. Even if your kid is having outburst after outburst for no apparent reason while every other kid seems to just roll with the punches, you can still welcome the storm. Of course, this is certainly easier said than done, so try not to be hard on yourself for any judgmental thoughts you happen to have.

Remember, if you are new to practicing mindfulness, trying to use this skill in emotionally charged moments may feel akin to learning to ride a bike on a steep incline. Thus, if you haven't already established a mindfulness practice during moments of calm, I recommend doing so now. Practicing some (if not all) of the mindfulness exercises listed in Chapter 3 when things are pleasant – both to begin with and on a regular basis – will make it easier to mindfully regard whatever stormy moments you encounter thereafter.

Alternatively, you can choose to reframe whatever judgmental thoughts happen to surface about your kids' emotional expressions, especially if adopting a nonjudgmental stance proves difficult. More specifically, consider the evidence for and against these judgmental thoughts, as well as how these thoughts are serving you. As a shortcut, here's a helpful reframe for some judgmental thoughts that might come up for you when with your kids. No, your kids aren't trying to make life difficult for you or anyone else. No, they aren't too sensitive or dramatic. And no, they aren't crybabies or delinquents. In fact, quite the opposite is true. Emotional outbursts are healthy and developmentally appropriate for children of all ages to have when dysregulated. Moreover, it is by going through these moments of dysregulation, however intense or messy they may be, that our kids – ideally with our help and support – eventually find their emotional equilibrium.

Suggestion 2: Stay Present-Focused

Aside from welcoming our kids' storms, one of the best ways to support our children (and ourselves) during their most heated moments is to focus on the present. Of course, when our kids are melting down, it's natural to jump to the future. Our worry that these kinds of outbursts will persist or even get worse leads us to try to clamp down on them in some way. We use the opportunity to teach our kids a lesson or problem-solve with them in hopes of preventing future storms, even though the current one is still raging, thus making it nearly impossible for our kids to take in any of what we are saying.

To clarify, I'm not suggesting that you have to accept that your kid will forevermore fall to the ground in tears whenever she doesn't get her way. With older kids, you very well may want to process and problem-solve with them after a meltdown to see if there might be changes one or both of you could make to reduce the frequency and intensity of future outbursts. However, the time for such an intervention is not during the storm or even after it has begun to die down, but rather once the clouds have finally parted.

Again, here is where mindfulness comes into play. Notice when your thoughts wander to the future (or even the past) and then come back to the present explosion or whatever you need to be doing as it unfolds. Keep doing this each time your mind travels to a different period and remember that all that's needed is getting through this one outburst, not the many that have come before it or those that have yet to come. And if you have an urge to turn the storm into a teachable moment, know that modeling how to stay in and accept – exactly as it is – such a challenging present is perhaps the most powerful lesson you could ever give your kids.

Suggestion 3: Get Curious

Although the two tips discussed thus far are natural extensions of the non-judgmental, present-moment acceptance that defines mindfulness, as noted previously, it's neither possible nor practical to be mindful 100 percent of the time. Moreover, true acceptance requires at least some understanding of that which we are trying to accept. Accordingly, when faced with our children's emotional eruptions, we can aim to strike a balance between accepting these exactly as they are and taking time to understand the forces that might be contributing to them. In other words, we can get curious, even as a storm is barreling toward us, and aim to identify the prompting event, thoughts, and vulnerability factors that might be giving rise to it. From there, we can intuit the most effective way to get through not only the storm in front of us but also its aftermath.

For example, instead of jumping to conclusions as to what's causing a given outburst, we can ask our kids or even just wonder aloud, especially if we didn't witness its onset. We might say, "Wow, you're so upset! I wonder what happened . . ." and see how our kids respond. We can then reflect whatever they share and ask open-ended questions to understand more, if needed.

To illustrate, let's say Jane walks into her living room and sees her four-year-old son, Zack, pointing at his little sister while shouting through tears, "She's playing with Mr. Bear!" Assuming Zack doesn't usually appear to have a strong attachment to the bear in his sister's arms, Jane might respond by saying, "Huh, she's playing with Mr. Bear and you don't like that! Tell me more. What makes that so upsetting?" She can then validate whatever sentiment is shared. For instance, she might respond by saying, "Ahh, you wanted to play with Mr. Bear but you can't because Maisy has him. How upsetting!"

Of course, not all children will be able or willing to share what triggered a particular emotion or why. However, asking these kinds of questions, even to the youngest of kids, helps us adopt a more curious and accepting stance and fosters in our kids the introspection needed for building emotional intelligence.

Similarly, we can take time to explore possible vulnerability factors that might be propelling the current storm, especially if our child's reaction seems disproportionate to the prompting event or if there doesn't seem to be a clear prompting event. As discussed in Chapter 4, in addition to considering recent and more distant stressors that might be making our children particularly vulnerable to experiencing intense emotions, we can also consider whether they have adequately fueled, moved, and rested their bodies. After all, none of us are at our best when we're lacking in one or more of these basic needs, and sometimes just recognizing this can go a long way toward helping us be more accepting of the explosion in front of us.

To be clear, I'm not encouraging trying to quiet our kids' storms by shoving food in their mouths or insisting that they drop and give us twenty push-ups or close their eyes on the spot. As a reminder, whether and how our kids choose to satisfy each of these needs is ultimately up to them. However, if we know that our kids are running low on any of these essentials and that this might be contributing to what we are seeing, then we can make these available at some point in the not-too-distant future. I can't tell you the number of times a meltdown has seemingly vanished in my own home once a healthy snack or meal was placed on the table for my kids. If nothing else, knowing that your kid is hungry, restless, or tired can help inform what you choose to do after the explosion. Maybe you have an earlier dinner or bedtime than usual or head to the playground for the afternoon instead of the movie theater. These simple adjustments really can be game changers on some days, clearing the way for much calmer weather . . . at least until the next storm hits.

Suggestion 4: Assume Nothing

The next tip dovetails with the last. Not only do we want to avoid making premature assumptions about the cause of a given storm, but we also want to avoid drawing unwarranted conclusions about its impact. Once again, we can get curious and use our mindfulness skills to observe the facts at hand and nothing more. The reason? I can't tell you the number of times I've seen a kid yank a toy out of another kid's hand only to see the "victim" happily move on to playing with another toy. In other words, just because we might be unhappy if someone did X, Y, or Z to us, doesn't mean that the affected child feels the same. Thus, just as we check in with kids who are struggling to regulate their emotions, we can check in (verbally or even just visually) with the children who happen to be in the path of another kid's outburst. And once again, when asking how these kids are feeling, we can use open-ended questions to avoid sending the message that they should be feeling a certain way. After all, kids are highly insightful and understand (at times better than us) that others sometimes say and do things when dysregulated that they wouldn't otherwise do. Put differently, why create a problem that doesn't exist?

Of course, if there is a problem, then we can validate and help the affected children, if needed. However, validation alone often does the trick. Indeed, contrary to what some might suggest, there's no need to scold or punish the dysregulated child in order to affirm those impacted by their behavior. Instead, we can convey support for all by validating any expressed feelings and by letting it be known that we're going to stay close for the duration of the storm to help keep everyone safe.

Suggestion 5: Hold Firm Limits

As noted in the previous chapter, it can be tempting to withdraw limits that prompt or seem to exacerbate our kids' emotional outbursts. However, caving in response to strong emotions teaches our kids that we aren't comfortable seeing them upset and that we're willing to let just about anything slide – even important expectations or rules – in order to get their storms to stop. Sure, the current meltdown may cease if we give in and allow our kids to skip a shower, watch extra TV, or do whatever it is we initially said no to. At the same time, however, our kids walk away from such experiences believing that exploding is an effective way to cope when they are dysregulated. The result? Even more dysregulated behavior!

To be clear, I strongly agree with Dr. Ross Greene that our children truly want to do well and aren't trying to manipulate us when they act out or protest our limits (Greene, 2016, 2021). Instead, as noted previously, I see these behaviors as a sign that our kids have been emotionally hijacked and need our help. At the same time, it's important to note that our responses to these unspoken (and often unrecognized) requests for assistance sometimes strengthen our children's challenging behaviors, thus making it more likely that these behaviors will reappear in the future.

To illustrate, let's say your son starts thrashing about when it's time to shower and you allow him to skip washing up once or twice in order to help him calm down, even though you typically hold this limit on other days. This is an example of what is known as partial or intermittent reinforcement because your son's behavior is only occasionally reinforced. Unfortunately, no matter how many times you hold this limit moving forward, your kid has learned (even if he doesn't consciously realize it) that thrashing about when he's dysregulated sometimes leads to you giving in. As a result, you can expect that this same behavior will likely continue to resurface whenever his executive center gets overwhelmed in the future; unless, of course, he is given the help he needs to enable him to be more skillful. This is because behaviors that are intermittently reinforced tend to be especially hard to break when reinforcement stops altogether due to the previously learned possibility that reinforcement very well may be just around the corner (Pittenger, 2002).

Thus, although you may occasionally choose to drop a limit you've set upon realizing it isn't really necessary or developmentally appropriate or realistic for one or more of your children, ideally these decisions will be well thought out (keeping in mind what we know about intermittent reinforcement), rather than knee-jerk reactions to your children's emotional displays or behaviors. Otherwise it's best, whenever possible, to confidently hold needed limits while welcoming your children's storms – even if they intensify in response. For example, you might say, "You really don't want to shower, I know! You got so sweaty today though, so it's time to take one. I'll get the water started for you." From there, you can aim to continue remaining warm but confident and firm – regardless of how your son responds – while staying nearby to help, as needed.

Suggestions for the Most Common Storms

While the prior tips can be used to help us navigate whatever blowups our children have, the ones that follow are specific to the most common ways these moments of emotional dysregulation manifest. And even though some outbursts may consist of every one of these behavioral manifestations, we'll consider recommendations for each of these separately given that these outward displays of emotion tend to evoke very different reactions in us.

Crying or Whining

Even if you follow each of the aforementioned suggestions, let's be honest . . . loud sobs and whines can still be incredibly grating on the ears. Whether we're feeling irked by our children's complaints and cries or sad to see them in such distress, it's normal to want to try to put an end to these unpleasant sounds. Yet, as noted previously, doing so is about as pointless as trying to stop the rain from falling, even if our children do quiet momentarily or even altogether. In fact, our attempts to placate our kids may come across to them as invalidating and unhelpful, and may even lead to more of the tears or howls that we were trying to halt in the first place. Thus, rather than try to pacify or reason with our kids when they are crying or complaining, we can, once again, welcome the storm – however discordant it may be. Of course, if our children want a hug or a soothing touch in these moments, we can certainly help them in these ways. However, it's best if the goal of these interventions is not to eliminate emotional pain but rather to support our kids as they navigate their distress.

Tantrums

Although most of us know a tantrum when we see one, the term is used rather loosely, and definitional discrepancies are not insignificant. Thus, when I speak of tantrums, I prefer to use a modified version of the definition Dr. Rebecca Hershberg gives in her book, *The Tantrum Survival Guide*. According to Dr. Hershberg, tantrums consist of acting-out behaviors that occur in response to not knowing how to manage or express an overwhelming emotional experience (Hershberg, 2018).[1] Of course, what one parent considers to be acting-out behaviors might be seen as par for the course in another parent's eyes. In other words, tantrums are inherently subjective.

Moreover, contrary to what many of us believe, tantrums are not limited to toddlerhood. In fact, even adults sometimes have full-blown tantrums. Thus, though I hate to be the bearer of bad news, your kids will likely have tantrums well into, and even past, their adolescent years.

Given this, let's talk about some tips for tantrums, specifically, aside from those noted earlier. Keeping in mind that a tantrum is a sign that the more primitive parts of our kids' brains have overpowered their executive centers, logical thinking and sound decision making are virtually impossible during such moments of dysregulation. Accordingly, a meltdown is not the time to try to reason with our kids or ask them to make choices, especially not difficult or complex ones. If, however, a choice needs to be made during a tantrum, it's best to limit any options given (no more than two is ideal) and to be prepared to make the decision for our kids, if necessary. Similarly, it's wise in these moments to be ready and willing, if needed, to help our kids complete tasks that they typically do independently, such as getting dressed or walking to the car. For instance, you might say, "Do you want to walk up the stairs or would you like me to carry you? Ah, it looks like you need some help, let me pick you up." It's also worth being prepared to physically stop our kids from doing things they wouldn't otherwise do, such as hitting, kicking, or biting. As an example, you might say, "Whoa! I can't let you bite me, but I can give you something else to bite if you'd like."

Critically, whatever we do or don't do during a tantrum, staying calm is the goal in order to avoid further taxing our children's already overwhelmed and dysregulated brains. Of course, we may, at times, have our own outburst right alongside our kids. That said, if we follow the storm survival tips given here and reach for the ART Tools to help us accept, regulate, and tolerate our emotions whenever our tempers start to climb, we'll have a much greater chance of keeping our cool and being the supportive and grounding force our kids need. More on this to come.

---

1 If you're willing, take a moment to consider how this non-judgmental definition feels in contrast to the judgmental way in which we typically use the word "tantrum." Do you notice a difference in your experience? If so, know that *that's* the power of non-judgmentally observing and describing reality.

Shouting and Hurtful Words

When caught in an emotional storm, it's not uncommon for our kids to shout and hurl hurtful words at us and others. Our kids might tell us that they hate us, that we stink, that we're the worst parent in the world, that we don't love them, that they'll never talk to us again, or even worse. Yet, however harsh these words may be, rest assured that they need not be taken at face value. Although it's possible that there's some truth in what our kids say during these heated exchanges, most often what they're really communicating – if we look beneath their words – is that they're feeling angry, hurt, ashamed, overwhelmed, or some other intensely painful emotion. They may even be so emotionally flooded that, in the moment, a part of them really believes whatever they're saying. Regardless, we can allow our kids to air these thoughts while focusing on the feelings driving them, knowing that they, too, will almost invariably dissipate along with the storm.

Having said that, it's worth noting that there may be times when our kids do little but shout and say hurtful things to us – as though they've been swept away by a perpetual storm.

For instance, when my son was five years old, he went through a months-long period where he would yell at me for no apparent reason, many times per day. Naturally, I was not immune to worries that this shouting might become a habit if I allowed it to continue. However, I also knew from the research of Dr. Louise Bates Ames, author of the book series *Your One-Year-Old* through *Your Ten- to Fourteen-Year-Old*, that it's common for kids to go through periods of disequilibrium, where their behavior is generally more challenging and brash than usual (Bates Ames et al., 1982, 1988). Given this, rather than insist that my son change his tone, I chose to accept his shouts while modeling the kind and polite way of speaking that I hoped he would one day adopt. Occasionally, when feeling particularly jarred by one of his angry demands, I would let him know that it might take me a moment longer than usual to get him the glass of water, the bagel, or whatever else it was that he wanted, because I really do freeze up a bit when yelled at by him or anyone else. However, aside from this, I aimed to graciously oblige whatever "requests" he made without trying to correct his approach. And what do you know? Somehow, the rather unpleasant phase we were stuck in ended almost as abruptly as it started, with modeling and time being the only explanations I can give for this shift.

Of course, accepting our kids' rude and unkind utterances in this way can be challenging, especially when someone else appears hurt by the words lobbed at them. For instance, would you really let your teenage son get away with telling his impressionable younger sister that she's fat and ugly when she's clearly crushed by the insult? For those who take a more conventional approach to parenting, the answer would almost certainly be a resounding "no." However, what if instead of scorning or shaming your son, you apologized for him and explained to your daughter that his anger led him to say things that aren't true, while also validating how hurt his words left her feeling? In doing so, you normalize how easy it is to say or do things we don't mean when upset, while also letting your daughter know that she doesn't deserve to be spoken to in that way. Remember, letting a storm blow over like this doesn't mean we can't circle back and discuss what happened at a later hour. In fact, if it were me, I'd plan to have a conversation with my son at some point after the fact about what he might do differently the next time he's angry with his sister and how I might be able to help. Yet, as always, I'd want to wait until we were back under more peaceful skies before going there.

The one exception to all of this would be if my kid were picking on another child (not a sibling with whom they have to coexist) who was visibly upset by my kid's taunts, in which case I'd want to put an end to this as quickly as possible by removing my child from the situations in which this was occurring. For example, a year or so before my son started shouting at me around the clock, I noticed that he was frequently teasing a slightly older cousin in a way that left his cousin feeling sad and hurt. Consequently, I informed my son that I wouldn't allow this to continue and that we would need to leave family gatherings early if and when this were to happen again. For the next few months, I shadowed him closely when we were with extended family, and when the taunting resurfaced (which it did only once), I lovingly and non-judgmentally picked him up and carried him to the car, where we sat until his dad and sister were ready to leave. Thankfully, that was the last time my son ever teased his cousin, and they are now best buds. Moreover, my son learned from this experience how much I value being kind and respectful to others, and he is now quite possibly one of the kindest kids you'll meet and truly a friend to all.

Dangerous or Destructive Behaviors

Finally, let's talk about what to do when our kids' emotional storms give way to dangerous or destructive behaviors. Although certainly not a comprehensive list, these acts may include things such as hitting, kicking, biting, throwing, head banging, scratching, cutting, and breaking toys or other objects. And as is the case with tantrums, which sometimes include these types of behaviors, hazardous actions are not limited to the toddler years. Indeed, even though we may see fewer of these behaviors as our kids age, the fact that our kids become stronger as they grow means that the risk for causing damage or harm with these behaviors increases over time. Hence the need, as always, for responding to the kid in front of you rather than the tinier person they used to be. In other words, what worked previously may not be as effective today.

Thankfully, with toddlers and younger kids, how to proceed is fairly straightforward given that they can't really pack a punch in the same way older children can. Having said that, even the youngest of kids can hurt others and break things, and it's on us to make sure that this doesn't happen – if we can. The key is to stay close when these types of behaviors are surfacing so that we can gently block them, validate the feelings underlying them, and offer safer, alternative ways for kids to release their feelings.

For instance, if your toddler is about to start throwing silverware upon learning that you will be serving pasta for dinner rather than the mac and cheese he demanded, you can calmly pick him up while gently prying the cutlery from his fingers and letting him know in a kind but firm voice that you won't let him throw things – especially hard or sharp things – at the dinner table. Meanwhile, you can compassionately acknowledge how upset he is that mac and cheese isn't an option for tonight's dinner and tell him that he doesn't have to eat if he doesn't want to. You might then offer to walk or carry him over to a sock drawer and allow him to throw as many socks as he'd like, while also letting him know that he's welcome to return to the table if and when he decides to join you for dinner.

Notice that nowhere in this example did I suggest scolding or punishing your son, withdrawing affection, or using anything other than calm and gentle hands as you escort him away from the table. And ideally, we can take a similar approach even when our little ones are hitting us, kicking a sibling, or engaging in other potentially harmful behaviors by physically stopping these behaviors for them. For example, if your child is hitting you while she's in your arms, you can calmly put her down while letting her know that you can't hold her if she's trying to hurt you. Or if she's attempting to kick a sibling, you can gently block these kicks with your hands while informing her (in a warm and matter-of-fact tone) that you won't let her do that.

On some occasions, we may need to check in with the recipient of these actions and provide comfort and assistance. Yet, even then, our job in these moments is still to welcome our dysregulated child's feelings without censure, while doing whatever's needed in order to keep them and others (including ourselves) safe. For instance, we may decide to remove our child from the situation or we may just choose to stay nearby. Once again, however, there's no need to try to eliminate the storm or drill into our child the many reasons why their behaviors aren't acceptable. Chances are, they already know that they shouldn't be doing what they're doing; they just don't have the ability to stop themselves when emotionally flooded and thus need us to help them find the brakes.

Of course, as our kids age, this becomes a little trickier given the potential for these kinds of acting-out behaviors to cause even greater damage or harm. That said, no matter how big our kids get, the advice of focusing on the feelings underlying dangerous or destructive behaviors while doing whatever's needed to keep everyone safe still holds. The only tweak here is that you may occasionally decide to remove a limit or expectation for the time being in order to avoid a further escalation that's likely to result in even more of these behaviors. Yep, that's right. Even though I generally recommend setting and holding firm limits in order to avoid inadvertently reinforcing challenging behaviors, sometimes making a game-time decision to drop these for the time being can actually be an effective way to ensure you aren't adding fuel to the fire. This is what Dr. Ross Greene calls Plan C in his Collaborative and Proactive Solutions (CPS) model (Greene & Winkler, 2019), which he outlines in his books, *Raising Human Beings* and *The Explosive Child* (Greene, 2016, 2021). The idea is to temporarily lift an expectation that your child is struggling to meet until you and your child have had a chance to work together to come up with a plan for how they can succeed when the expectation is reintroduced.

For instance, if your 13-year-old starts throwing her gear when you tell her it's time for soccer practice, you might let her play hooky for the day and make a mental note to revisit this with her another time. In other words, you can make a strategic decision to hold off on sending her to practice until the two of you have figured out what made getting ready so difficult, as well as what might make it easier the next time around. Maybe her cleats are too small, maybe her coach is being unkind to her, or maybe she is frustrated with her performance on the field. Whatever the issue may be, once identified, you can brainstorm together how to resolve it so that her cleats don't go flying whenever it's time to head to practice.

I encouraged Alice (the stressed-out mom of three boys I introduced in Chapter 3) to take a similar approach with her six-year-old after he kicked a hole in their living room wall. Rather than expect her son to entertain himself when she was playing with or helping one of his brothers (which had been the prompting event for the hole-in-the-wall incident), I suggested that she set her son up for success by allowing him to do something special during these times. Together, she and her six-year-old decided that he would get to listen to a podcast that he loved whenever Alice was busy playing with or helping one of his siblings for more than a few minutes. This turned out to work wonders as he was an avid podcast fan and began to look forward to pockets in the day where he could listen to his favorite shows without interruption from Alice or his brothers.

Notably, however, if dangerous or destructive behaviors persist or increase in frequency despite these efforts to troubleshoot, it may be worth seeking individualized, professional support. And if self-injurious behaviors such as cutting are involved, help from a mental health professional should be sought as soon as possible.

Navigating Our Own Emotional Storms

As if our children's emotional storms aren't enough for us to contend with, we as parents also must traverse our own complicated inner worlds. The silver lining of this reality, however, is that we are unlikely to ever run out of opportunities to practice relating more skillfully to painful emotions. Moreover, when we manage to navigate our own challenging emotions without letting how we feel compromise our interactions with those we love, we not only leave behind a map for our kids of how to one day do the same, but we also avert the storms that our own words and actions might otherwise provoke within them. After all, our kids are, in many ways, like sponges and can detect even the slightest changes in our moods. Thus, the more we can anchor ourselves and commit to acting in accord with our values in the midst of our own distress, the less likely it is that our kids will absorb whatever vibes we may be emitting.

Unfortunately, so often when we are feeling intense, painful emotions, we go on autopilot, doing whatever our emotions beg us to do without giving much thought to the consequences of our actions. Even if we think what we are doing is logical or necessary, when caught in our own emotional storms, there's a good chance we're actually just ceding control to our emotions. Only once the storm has passed do we realize there might have been a better way forward.

Given this, one of the most important things we can do when feeling strong, unwanted emotions – whether with our kids or not – is to slow down and proceed with caution. When you are about to say or do something in a moment of anger, anxiety, frustration, or disappointment, pause for a moment before proceeding. Take a break from the situation by grabbing a glass of water, going to the bathroom, or if it's safe to do so, taking a walk before returning to your kids or whomever else you are interacting with. Spend this time mindfully noticing your thoughts and feelings, or if that proves too difficult, your surroundings. Remind yourself of what kind of parent you want to be and what kind of relationship you want to have with your kids and consider what's going to be most effective in helping you achieve these long-term goals. Then, from this more centered place, proceed tactfully using the ART Tools, as needed, to help you accept, regulate, and tolerate your emotions. In case it helps, a list of each of these skills is included in Table 7.1 for your reference.

Table 7.1 Accepting, regulating, and tolerating our own emotional storms with the ART Tools.

---

1) **Mindfully notice what's going on within or outside of you, including any of the following:**

- The rise and fall of your chest as you breathe
- Your feet touching the ground when sitting or walking
- The thoughts in your mind (just remember not to latch onto these or treat them as facts!)
- The sounds around you (e.g., the sound of the rain falling on the roof)
- The sights around you (e.g., the painting on the wall, the cars passing by)
- Your children's facial expressions and body language

2) **Problem-solve to change the prompting event**

- For instance, if you're stressed about tasks that need to be done, create a plan for how you will complete these, enlisting help from others as needed.
- Or, if you're overwhelmed by the mess that your kids are creating in the house, bring them outside for a bit or somewhere that isn't your home. Libraries, play gyms, and children's museums are all great for days when you can't stand the thought of one more bin being dumped on the floor.

3) **Decrease emotional vulnerability**

- Have you fueled, moved, and rested your body recently? If not, consider doing so as soon as possible.
  - Even if you can't go for a run, consider stretching your body, running in place, doing jumping jacks, or having a dance party with your kids. Likewise, even if you don't have time to make a meal or take a nap, grab a nourishing snack that you can eat on the go or ask a friend or family member for help so you can have some time to catch up on sleep.

4) **Reframe unhelpful thoughts**

- Ask yourself the following:
  - What's the evidence for and against these thoughts?
  - How are these thoughts serving you?
- Use your answers to these questions to come up with alternative, more realistic and useful thoughts.

(Continued)

Table 7.1 (Continued)

---

5) **Use the CARE skills**

- Cool with ice – submerge your head in a bowl of cold water or put an ice pack over your eyes, upper cheeks, and temples for 20–30 seconds.
- Activate your body – engage in 20 minutes of intense, aerobic exercise.
- Relax your muscles – tense individual muscle groups for 3–4 seconds and then release these muscles, paying attention to how it feels to let go of the tension.
- Exhale slowly – breathe in for 3–4 seconds, out for 7–8 seconds, and then hold your breath for 3–4 seconds before taking the next inhalation.

6) **Practice opposite action**

- Do the opposite of whatever you feel like doing when acting on these urges wouldn't be helpful.
  - For instance, if you feel like saying something hurtful, consider speaking lovingly and respectfully instead. Alternatively, you can choose to say nothing at all.

7) **Distract and self-soothe**

- Let the storm rage within while you focus your attention elsewhere, possibly even on something that may give rise to an entirely different emotion.
- Soothe yourself by focusing on comforting sights, sounds, smells, tastes, or touches.

Naturally, weathering intense emotional storms sometimes requires using multiple skills. Thus, try using one ART Tool at a time for a few minutes and see how you feel. If your level of arousal is still high, see what happens when you use another skill and then another, and keep trying different ones until you feel confident that you can get through the moment without doing something you'll later regret. As a reminder, although the fast-acting CARE skills rapidly reduce arousal, their effects tend to be temporary. Thus, it's important to follow these with additional skills once you've gotten your executive center back online.

Of note, if you'd prefer to get some distance from your kids before turning to these skills, let them know that you're struggling and need to take some time to find your center – ideally while making it clear that your feelings are your responsibility, not theirs. Remember, it's okay if your kids aren't thrilled to see you step away. Caring for yourself doesn't require your children's permission or approval.

Relatedly, please know that it's okay for your children to occasionally see you upset and not at your best. When they do, you can be honest with them and let them know that you're having a hard time and – if you wish – why that's the case. For instance, following a recent second-trimester miscarriage that left me heartbroken, angry, and not myself for weeks on end, I was noticeably more distracted than usual when with my kids and cried in front of them on multiple occasions. However, each time they saw me consumed by my grief, I let them know that my tears had nothing to do with them but were instead a result of our loss. In other words, I made it clear that they were not responsible for my feelings, just as I try to do even when their behavior prompts an uncomfortable emotion in me. After all, no matter how many buttons my kids push, whether I allow these buttons to light up is entirely within my control, even when it doesn't feel like that's the case.

Weathering Simultaneous Emotional Storms

Of all the challenging moments that we face as parents, perhaps most ominous are the ones when we end up being every bit as dysregulated as our children. It is in these moments that we are most likely to say or do something that will weaken our connection with our kids and become one of the greatest hits to replay again and again on the regret track of our minds. Instead of heeding the conditions and focusing on calming ourselves, we make impulsive, frantic efforts to try to control our kids, forgetting that we have skills to help us get through the moment that they have not yet acquired. As a result, we demand that our children pull themselves together even though we are unable to do so ourselves. Unfortunately, this approach almost always backfires, causing the storm to rage more intensely within and around us and our children.

The good news, however, is that these days don't have to end with us crying ourselves to sleep. If we can remember that our children's storms will not settle until we find a way to settle ourselves, then we can shift our efforts toward decreasing our own arousal so that we can be the calming force our kids need. What's more, you've already learned all the skills that are required to get through these especially challenging moments. So, rather than repeat the ART Tools and tips that are available for you to use, let's bring these to life with a vignette of a family whose storms are on the verge of colliding.

***

Layla and her four kids arrived home after a long day out of the house on what felt, to Layla, like day 50 of her kids' two-week winter break. In reality, it was day 11. Although she had taken time off to be with her kids, she was hoping to make partner in the New Year and felt uneasy about being out of the office for so long. Plus, even though she was technically on vacation, emails and calls from clients and colleagues continued to stream in, and she felt obligated to respond to these in whatever spare moments she could find. Although this particular day had initially been fun for all, her kids started bickering (yet again) on the car ride home. Oh, and did I mention that her partner was traveling for work, leaving her flying solo? Needless to say, Layla was feeling drained and more than ready for her kids to return to school and their usual schedules.

And yet, here she was, with three more days left to go alone with her kiddos and lots of grumbling in the background, which – given the late hour – she took to be a sign that her kids were hungry for dinner. She therefore set to work preparing the night's meal while her kids went their separate ways to play and unwind from the day. As she was cooking, she pulled out her phone to catch up on some work emails, distracting her from the stir fry on the stove. A few minutes later, her eldest daughter, Mia, started shouting angrily as she chased her visibly frightened sisters around the house. Exasperated by what seemed to be her kids' near-constant fighting and wanting to prevent things from escalating even more, Layla left the kitchen to try to stop the brawl, just in time to see Mia land a blow on her little sister's tiny head. Four-year-old Kaya immediately crumpled to the floor and began sobbing as Layla scooped her up and gave her a big hug. Anger now fully bubbling within Layla, she was about to reprimand Mia for hurting her sister when her son called out, "it smells like something is burning!"

Seconds later, the smoke alarm went off and Layla returned to the kitchen to find the stir fry completely scorched. Although her girls had stopped fighting at the sound of the alarm, all four kids were now complaining about the fact that dinner was ruined and were insisting that they needed food, stat! Heart pounding and feeling as though she was about to explode, Layla turned off the stove and opened some windows in hopes of airing out the kitchen and silencing the blaring beeps of the alarm. This seemed to do the trick – for the alarm at least – and Layla breathed a sigh of relief to have one less sound to contend with. And somehow, in that tiny reprieve, Layla found herself able to pause and think a little more clearly. Recognizing that she was on the brink of discharging her anger in a way that would likely only further dysregulate her kids and leave her feeling worse, she decided to use her ART Tools to help her accept, regulate, and tolerate her emotions so she could get through the moment more skillfully.

First, she took a few seconds to practice acceptance by mindfully notic-ing what was going on in her body, while allowing her kids' gripes to exist in the background. In doing so, she made the following observations, both of which helped guide her next steps: 1) she was starving; and 2) her body was incredibly tense. Armed with this information and the undeniable hun-ger of her kids, Layla opened the fridge to see what she might be able to quickly cobble together while briefly tensing and then releasing the mus-cles in her body in order to help relax them, thus cooling her arousal so she could better tolerate the moment. Since she knew time was of the essence as their bodies clearly needed fuel to help them regulate, she decided to cre-ate and serve a smorgasbord of leftovers from the past few nights' dinners. Within five or so minutes, she and the kids were eating and their storms seemed to be lifting, although she still felt on edge and knew they weren't fully in the clear just yet.

Accordingly, she decided to practice opposite action in order to help her tolerate these feelings and ensure they wouldn't get the better of her. Instead of acting on her lingering angry urges to scold, lecture, or blame her kids for the burnt supper and negative energy they had brought to the eve-ning, she lovingly kissed each child's head as she cleaned up the table and expressed gratitude for the various ways in which each of them had helped her or each other that day. Then, even though Layla and her kids were all in much better spirits, she figured some self-soothing couldn't hurt, so she put on some Disney tunes while they ate dessert to help them tolerate whatever emotional aftereffects might be present.

To her surprise, bedtime went smoother than ever that night, though Layla knew how very different the evening would have looked had she given in to the unhelpful urges she'd been having just moments prior. And while fully aware that she wouldn't always navigate simultaneous storms with such grace, she felt not only immensely proud of herself for using the ART Tools to salvage the evening, but also better prepared to face whatever might come in the future.

Parenting Exercise

Now it's your turn! Practice accepting, regulating, and tolerating your children's emotions and your own using the strategies and skills outlined in this chapter. For quick reference, see the list of all of the ART Tools (provided earlier in this chapter in Table 7.1) that you can use to navi-gate your own emotional storms. In addition, here's a brief summary of the

ART-informed suggestions I gave for moments when your kids are emotionally dysregulated:

1) Welcome the storm
   - Remember that trying to push back against our kids' emotions is about as pointless (and exhausting!) as trying to keep away the rain by holding buckets up to the sky in the middle of a downpour. Instead, we're much better off non-judgmentally accepting our children's storms while reframing or shifting our attention away from any judgmental thoughts that happen to arise so we can return to mindfully noticing the moment exactly as it is.

2) Stay present-focused
   - Mindfully observe the present outburst while resisting any urges to think about prior or future explosions. If your mind does wander to the past or future, remember that all that's needed is getting through this one, challenging moment as you gently shift your attention back onto the present.

3) Get curious
   - Aim to identify the prompting event and vulnerability factors that may have given rise to your children's emotional storms and respond contingently. If your kids haven't fueled, moved, and rested their bodies recently, consider adjusting your plans in order to help them meet these basic needs.

4) Assume nothing
   - Mindfully notice or check in with others who might be impacted by your dysregulated child's behavior, validating and helping anyone who happens to be in distress.

5) Hold firm limits
   - Unless a limit you've set isn't necessary or developmentally appropriate, hold firm limits while welcoming any outbursts that your children may have in response. If you do occasionally decide to withdraw a needed limit, make sure this is a conscious choice and be prepared to accept the potential consequences of this intermittent reinforcement.

Most importantly, know that it's okay if all of this feels unnatural or challenging to remember in the moment. If you haven't discovered this already, mastering these tools and strategies is anything but easy. That said, I encourage you to take advantage of any and all opportunities to practice implementing these skills and suggestions, knowing that the more you do so, the more skillful you will likely become at relating to whatever uncomfortable feelings you encounter on your journey as a parent.

References

Bates Ames, L., Ilg, F. L., & Baker, S. (1988). *Your ten- to fourteen-year-old*. Dell Publishing.

Bates Ames, L., Ilg, F. L., & Haber, C. C. (1982). *Your one-year-old: The fun-loving, fussy 12–24-month-old*. Dell Publishing.

Casey, B. J., Jones, R. M., & Hare, T. A. (2008). The adolescent brain. *Annals of the New York Academy of Sciences, 1124*, 111–126. https://doi.org/10.1196/annals.1440.010

Greene, R. (2016). *Raising human beings: Creating a collaborative partnership with your child*. Scribner.

Greene, R. (2021). *The explosive child: A new approach for understanding and parenting easily frustrated, chronically inflexible children* (6th ed.). Harper Collins.

Greene, R., & Winkler, J. (2019). Collaborative & proactive solutions (CPS): A review of research findings in families, schools, and treatment facilities. *Clinical Child and Family Psychology Review, 22*(4), 549–561. https://doi.org/10.1007/s10567-019-00295-z

Hershberg, R. S. (2018). *The tantrum survival guide: Tune into your toddler's mind (and your own) to calm the craziness and make family fun again*. The Guilford Press.

Pittenger, D. J. (2002). The two paradigms of persistence. *Genetic, Social, and General Psychology Monographs, 128*(3), 237–268.

When We've Lost Our Bearings and Gone Astray

8

Overcoming Obstacles and Learning From Mistakes

In case this message hasn't hit home just yet, there is no such thing as a perfect parent. Although the strategies discussed thus far will hopefully help you to skillfully weather the emotional storms that come your way, you will likely still find yourself rattled by your kids' behaviors at times and will almost certainly lose your cool every now and then when with your children. After all, at the risk of repeating myself one too many times, parenting is an incredibly demanding and challenging job and inevitably involves making mistakes, even for the most emotionally savvy among us.

Thankfully, these mistakes don't mean that we are bad parents. Instead, these humbling moments remind us that we are fallible, just like our kids, and provide an opportunity for us to apologize non-defensively to them and acknowledge that we could have been kinder, more patient, and less reactive. Further, these slips can function as reminders to pause and reflect on our own behavior in order to understand what factors led us astray and how we might do better down the road. With this in mind, let's start by taking a look at some of the most common barriers to Emotion-Savvy Parenting, as well as science-informed strategies for overcoming these, before discussing how to get back on track when we've veered off course.

DOI: 10.4324/9781003428343-12

Ambivalence or Misunderstanding of the Approach

As any salesperson can tell you, the sales pitch is everything. If you don't believe that the car you are considering purchasing is the car for you, chances are you are going to walk away. Of course, the same goes here. Even if you mostly buy into the ideas presented thus far, if there's even a seed of doubt as to whether this approach is right for you and your family, adopting this new way of parenting may prove to be difficult at times – especially when intense, uncomfortable emotions are on board.

To be clear, I would be shocked if you didn't sometimes question this new way of relating to your kids. For instance, you may wonder if your kids will really grow into the emotionally agile people you hope they'll become if you continue giving them room to feel their emotions in full, no matter how unskillful they come across in the process. As a result, you may find yourself on the fence every now and then (or more) as to how to proceed. Maybe your therapist or your child's therapist is recommending a different approach. Or maybe your kids are neurodivergent and you're unsure as to whether this approach will help them develop the skills they need to be successful.

While I could try to reassure you in one way or another that Emotion-Savvy Parenting is the way to go no matter your circumstances, doing so would likely only go so far – assuaging your mind temporarily, if that. Inevitably, the thought "What if she's wrong?" would likely surface, reopening the floodgates of doubt. And to be honest, there's no way to know for sure. There haven't been any head-to-head comparisons between Emotion-Savvy Parenting and more traditional parenting styles. Plus, even if we had solid data demonstrating that this approach is the most effective way to parent, that wouldn't tell us all that much about the ideal method for you or your family. In other words, there's no guarantee that a different style wouldn't work better in your home.

Thankfully, there's no need to go searching for certainty here. Instead, we can embrace the uncertainty that comes with parenting and accept that the voices in our heads *might* be right. Maybe this approach isn't right for us and our kids. Maybe. Yet, just because this is a possibility, doesn't mean we have to act as though it's a fact. Indeed, if we throw in the towel every time this doubt arises, we'll never know what might have happened had we stayed the course. This is the only guarantee I can really give you. If you abandon ship in the face of ambivalence, this approach most certainly won't "work" in your home. We'll talk about how to measure success shortly, but before we do, let's clear up a few common misconceptions about Emotion-Savvy Parenting that may be fueling some skepticism.

First, contrary to what many assume, welcoming feelings isn't permissive. Remember, we're not condoning or reinforcing unsafe, destructive, or inappropriate behavior when taking a respectful, emotion-savvy approach to parenting. Quite the opposite: We're setting limits to prevent this kind of behavior in the first place and blocking it when it does occur, all while accepting the thoughts and feelings that are driving it. Permissive parenting is what unfolds when we fear our kids' internal worlds so much that we opt to forgo setting or holding needed limits in hopes of preventing the "uglier" of our kids' thoughts and feelings from spilling out into the open. Sure, we could take a more authoritarian approach and try to police both our kids' behaviors and their feelings, but doing so wouldn't get rid of the feelings altogether. If anything, it would likely only make them more intense and more disruptive when they inevitably escape.

Another concern may be that Emotion-Savvy Parenting appears too hands-off. However, in truth, it's hands-on where it matters and hands-off where it doesn't matter so much, or where a more hands-on approach might be counter-productive to our goals. No, you may not get any brownie points when you are the only parent at the children's museum not on the floor "teaching" your children how to play, but you will be saving valuable energy by choosing to either mindfully observe or mindfully participate instead. You'll also get a much better glimpse of how the world looks through your children's eyes when you aren't the one making all the play calls, while also setting them up to become the independent, self-directed people we all hope our kids will one day grow to be.

A final concern I sometimes hear is that the approach I've described in this book precludes the kind of open and honest communication valued by most of us. Yet, while it's true that composing ourselves in the face of strong feelings isn't fully transparent or authentic, doing so allows us to act in line with our most deeply held values and gives our kids the space and freedom needed to be their authentic selves. If we were to voice every thought and feeling we have while acting on the urges that come with these, we would (inadvertently or not) likely shut down our kids' attempts to share their inner experiences with us. As a result, we'd essentially be leaving our kids to fend for themselves in the face of overpowering emotions, rather than connecting with them and helping their developing brains learn how to ride the waves of these feelings.

What's more, as the old adage goes, actions speak louder than words. We can tell our kids all day long how important it is to control their behaviors, but if we don't do so ourselves, why should they? Instead, we can model the behavior we hope to one day see, creating maps for our kids of more skillful, socially acceptable ways of managing strong emotions – all while trusting that eventually, with many years of brain development on their side, they will likely become every bit as adept as us (if not more so) at navigating emotional storms.

A Faulty Barometer for Success

So, let's get back to the question of how to measure success. What exactly does successful parenting look like? Many of us assume that if our kids are well-behaved, then we must be doing this parenting thing right. By contrast, if our kids are "misbehaving," then we're clearly missing the mark somehow. Although this isn't necessarily the case, if even a part of us believes that it is, we might be tempted to give up and revert to traditional parenting tactics at the first sign of non-compliance. After all, we all want to raise kids who are kind, empathic, successful, well-mannered, and independent, and it can be incredibly challenging to trust that these adjectives will one day describe our kids when they act in ways that are so out of sync with what we hope to see. Given this, it can be easy to let fear get the best of us and lead us to jump on our kids to do better in these moments.

As noted previously, however, limit testing is not only to be expected but is also an indicator of healthy development – and for good reason. Kids learn a tremendous amount about us, themselves, and the world by testing limits and getting answers to questions such as the following: How will my parents respond if I climb the wall that they told me not to climb? Will they stop me from doing so again or give in and let me climb it? Can I physically even scale the wall? What will I find on the other side if I reach the top?

Learning aside, limit testing is also a sign that our kids' brains are still developing, as will continue to be the case even through early adulthood (Casey et al., 2008). Indeed, kids often test limits simply because their executive centers aren't yet mature enough to inhibit urges from the more primitive, impulsive parts of their brains. For example, whereas we might be able to resist the urge to speed while driving, our teens may struggle to do the same due to weakened control from their developing executive centers.

This tends to be especially true at the end of a long day outside of the home, as our kids' executive centers have to work extra hard to conform to the strict rules and social expectations that are typically found in schools, summer camps, and extracurricular activities. Overworked and overtired, their executive centers essentially go offline when they get home, resulting in limit testing galore. Termed "after-school restraint collapse" by parenting educator Andrea Loewen Nair, this fatigue can give way to some very challenging, unpleasant behaviors (Loewen Nair, 2016). Critically, however, these behaviors are not a reflection of poor parenting, but are instead a sign that our kids feel comfortable enough with us to finally stop straining their overly taxed brains. Conversely, if our kids don't feel safe testing limits at home, their executive centers might easily go offline at school or in other out-of-home settings as a result of working so hard to keep their behaviors in check at home. Unfortunately, this may result in our kids getting branded as troublemakers when really, their executive centers are simply too fried to exert the control that's needed in these environments.

That said, it's worth noting that some children are wired to test more than others and may engage in limit testing both in and out of the home, regardless of how we respond to their behaviors. Others may hardly test limits at all, with us or anyone else. Given this, our kids' behaviors aren't really the best indicator of how we are doing as parents. Instead, what matters is how we respond to our children's feelings and behaviors. Are we frequently getting frazzled and trying to exert control over things that aren't really ours to control? Or are we mostly remaining calm (at least outwardly) while setting and holding needed limits and welcoming whatever feelings follow? Although the latter approach does often give way to less limit testing than the former, this isn't always the case. Either way, remember that we're playing the long game as parents, leaving behind blueprints for our children in every interaction we have with them. Thus, once again, it is our behaviors (rather than our kids') that ought to serve as our barometer for success.

Intense Emotional Arousal

Obviously, controlling our own behaviors is easier said than done, particularly when we're flooded with intense, painful emotions. In these moments, it can be difficult to remember that we have skills we can use to deescalate our climbing tempers. Plus, even if we're conscious of the fact that these skills are available to us, our heated state can make it incredibly challenging to actually use them. This is what Dr. Marsha Linehan calls our "skills breakdown point" (Linehan, 2015).

Having said that, though we may sometimes give in to unhelpful urges when experiencing extreme emotional arousal, the more we practice using distress tolerance skills when we aren't particularly heated, the more likely it is that we'll be able to utilize these skills in more intense moments. What's more, each time we turn to these skills in the face of powerful emotions, we increase our odds of doing so again the next time we find ourselves emotionally flooded.

Of course, we can also utilize the emotion regulation skills outlined in Chapter 4 to reduce our vulnerability to experiencing intense emotional arousal in the first place. Yet, whether we take a preventive or reactive approach to managing these emotions, practice will only take us so far.

No matter how much we practice being skillful, we will *all* inevitably succumb to the urges that accompany strong feelings at one point or another. This is where acceptance and self-compassion come into play, as well as the chain and solution analyses discussed later in this chapter. Once again, giving in to unhelpful urges when emotionally charged doesn't make us bad parents. It's just a humble reminder that we're human and need to keep practicing our skills in hopes of doing better the next time around. Thankfully, when it comes to parenting, there's just about always a next time.

Judgments From Others

For many, one of the greatest barriers to parenting in the respectful, emotionally attuned way I've described is the fear of judgment from others who subscribe to more traditional parenting approaches. Maybe you'd like to embrace Emotion-Savvy Parenting but worry that others will judge you and think you are ineffective or weak for parenting in this unorthodox way. Or maybe you're sold on this method when at home but cave and resort to using more conventional parenting strategies whenever you find yourself parenting in public in hopes of avoiding scrutiny. Wherever you fall in this regard, please know that I have had similar concerns (and still do at times) and that these are perfectly understandable given our society's norms regarding child-rearing. Unfortunately, our desire to parent as others think we should can easily lead us astray and make it hard to be the parents we want to be. Indeed, as I was reminded not too long ago in my personal life, it takes a lot of courage and resolve to parent in this radically different way when you know that those around you would do things differently. Here's the story:

While gathering with a large group of family for dinner, my brother-in-law asked me to sit at the kitchen table with his 18-month-old daughter while he grabbed a plate of food. The moment he got up, my niece started crying loudly, clearly upset that her dad was no longer by her side. Although there were many adults in the room, I was the one closest to my niece, so all eyes turned to me to see how I would respond to her cries. Logically, I knew that the kindest, most compassionate response would be to allow my niece to voice her displeasure in full, and yet, aware of the fact that the spotlight was on me, I felt a tremendous pull to try to "fix" her feelings. Instead, I sat by her side while softly speaking something along the following lines: "Oh, I know, you really want your dad and are upset that he's not here." In response, my niece began crying even louder, causing even more eyes to turn my way. Cheeks flushed and feeling very self-conscious and aware that people were likely wondering why I wasn't soothing her in some way, I continued: "He's grabbing some food for dinner and he'll be back in a minute, but I can see it's hard waiting for him. I totally get it."

Miraculously, though I was not in any way trying to stifle her tears, my niece looked at me as I spoke these words, nodded her head, and happily began eating the cut-up pieces of food on the tray in front of her. Amazement ensued. Had anyone else been sitting next to my niece, they likely would have picked her up and distracted her out of her tears, but it turned out that all she really needed was someone to quietly empathize with her and give her space to feel and express herself.

That said, I don't know how things would have played out had she not settled as quickly as she did. Without a doubt, my urges to soothe my niece would have increased had she continued crying, and I can only hope that I would have been strong enough to stay the course, despite the negative evaluations that would have almost surely followed. However, even if I had continued welcoming my niece's cries, my guess is that someone else likely would have swooped in to try to help, quieting her with some kind of silly song or game in a matter of seconds. After all, it's hard not intervening in these ways, especially if we believe it's our job to pacify any cries our kids emit.

Likewise, it can be every bit as challenging to resist giving in to the urge to force our kids to adhere to social conventions when around others. For example, Jake, the father of four who you met at the end of Chapter 5, shared that his anxiety pulled for him to insist that his kids apologize and say "thank you" when socially expected, no matter how they were feeling on the inside. As is the case for most of us, he didn't want others to think that he and his kids were impolite, though he acknowledged that he was more concerned in these situations with his reputation than that of his kids. At the same time, he admitted that these forced expressions from his kids often came across as inauthentic, which made sense given that they tended to be at odds with how his kids were actually feeling in the moment. Indeed, it's not really possible to give a genuine, heart-felt apology when seething internally.

Accordingly, Jake and I discussed dropping these demands that he'd been putting on his kids and replacing these with his own sincere expressions. For instance, instead of forcing his daughter to say "I'm sorry" on the playground, I encouraged him to apologize for her, saying something such as, "I'm sorry my daughter yelled at you back there." Similarly, rather than tell his kids to say thank you for gifts that they clearly didn't like, I suggested Jake say thank you for them.

As you might imagine, this was very difficult for Jake at first. He felt uncomfortable letting his kids off the hook in these situations and knew that others might be judging him for this. However, the more he practiced focusing on his response, rather than that of his kids, the easier it became to do so. What's more, occasionally this modeling seemed to pay off. Although by no means masters of social etiquette, every now and then Jake's kids would beat him to the punch, giving a meaningful apology or expressing heartfelt gratitude before he even had a chance to do so for them.

As Jake and other parents I work with (myself included) have learned, the best way to navigate concerns about what others might think of our parenting is simply to accept that they may not approve of what we do or don't do. In other words, rather than parent from a place of fear, we can instead allow for the possibility of being judged while choosing to do what we believe is best for ourselves and our kids. And the truth is, no matter what approach we follow when parenting, we'll never please everyone. Thankfully, that's not our job.

Partners With Divergent Views

For better or worse, one job that does come with the territory for many of us is partnering with a spouse, family member, and/or co-parent to raise our kids. Unfortunately, when another caregiver believes in using conventional parenting tactics, veering away from these in favor of a more respectful approach can be tricky. This clash of styles may result in heightened emotional arousal for all, as well as intense relationship conflict, thereby making it harder to show up as we'd like for our kids. It may also give rise to a sense of urgency in us to try to convince the other caregiver to join our side.

Admittedly, it would be much easier for all if our partners and co-parents – as well as our kids' grandparents, nannies, and teachers – also took an emotionally savvy approach to interacting with our children. However, the good news is that we (and our kids) can still reap the benefits of this approach even if the other adults in our kids' lives use more traditional child-rearing methods. Plus, if we are skillful and patient, we might even convince our partner (or our children's other caregivers) to join our side, as Shayna, a mom of four kids, eventually came to discover.

For years, Shayna and her partner, Liam, argued over how to best manage their kids' behaviors, as well as their own. Liam firmly believed that punishments and harsh, stern voices were needed in order to deal with misbehavior, and he considered his angry and annoyed expressions justified responses to whining, tantrums, non-compliance, and most other forms of wrongdoing. Although Shayna also struggled to keep her cool at times when with their kids, she recognized that this wasn't helpful and mostly believed it was on her (not her kids) to do better.

Regrettably, their differing perspectives resulted in many arguments over the years. Convinced that a unified front was needed at all times, Liam would get upset when Shayna chose to not back him up or told the kids that they didn't deserve to be yelled at by him or anyone else. Shayna, on the other hand, felt exasperated by what she saw as Liam's constant undoing of her hard work to welcome her kids' feelings and regulate her own, and she worried about the emotional harm his temper might cause. Ironically, though she was fairly skilled at not scolding the kids, she seemed to think Liam was a fair and deserving target for her anger and frustration and repeatedly blamed him for amplifying the chaos and tension in their home – not recognizing how, in doing so, she was only fanning the flames.

Luckily, Shayna and Liam have come a long way, thanks in large part to Liam pointing out that he could benefit from the same grace Shayna gives their kids. Once Shayna stopped criticizing Liam for his every misstep, he became much more open to hearing her perspective. Over the course of many shame-free conversations and interactions, Liam's conventional beliefs started to unravel, and he began looking for tools and strategies to help him become a more emotionally savvy parent. To this end, he began working with a therapist to help him better regulate his own emotions and he has made remarkable gains in this regard – so much so that he and Shayna are now mostly on the same page when it comes to parenting.

Of course, they don't always see eye to eye, and Liam still struggles to maintain his composure when with their kids on a fairly regular basis. That said, Shayna has learned that approaching these differences and setbacks in the same way she approaches challenges with her kids (i.e., nonjudgmentally and collaboratively) works much better than pointing fingers and demanding change. Recognizing that Liam is doing the best he can with the tools that he currently has – just as we all are – has helped Shayna be more patient when he isn't able to keep his cool. No, they aren't perfect; however, they are a much stronger team than ever before and now help each other be the parents they both want to be. When one of them starts to become heated, the other jumps in (without judgment) to help. And when an interaction doesn't go the way one or both of them would have liked, they debrief together to see what they might do differently the next time they find themselves in a similar situation.

Having said that, please know that it's common for daylight to exist between partners when it comes to parenting and that some couples struggle more than others to resolve these differences (if they ever do). Although you can't force your partner to change, you can take steps to help bridge any gaps between the two of you. Perhaps most important, you can use the ART Tools to be as skillful as possible whenever disagreements about your approaches to parenting arise. Resist urges to judge or criticize your partner (especially in front of your kids) and instead aim to be a source of support and understanding. If your partner is criticizing you for taking a more emotionally savvy approach to parenting, try to hear and address their concerns while staying calm, standing your ground, and modeling what you hope to one day see from them. You may also want to consider seeking couples or individual therapy (for you or your partner), especially if your divergent views on parenting are causing you distress or straining your relationship. Alternatively, you can encourage your partner to read this book or listen to podcasts about gentler, more respectful approaches to parenting, while keeping in mind that whether they choose to take you up on these suggestions is entirely up to them.

For those of you who happen to be reading this book at the request of your partner, way to go! It takes a tremendous amount of courage to be willing to consider the possibility that there might be a more effective way to parent, so hats off to you for doing so!

Overcoming Obstacles

Although I've hopefully convinced you by now to embrace this new way of relating to the emotions you encounter as a parent, you will likely stray at times from the path paved here. Thankfully, whether you find yourself off track due to one of the obstacles just mentioned or for an entirely different reason, there's always a way to return to this skillful, more peaceful way of parenting. In fact, noticing that you've veered off course and trying to find your way back is an example of Emotion-Savvy Parenting in and of itself, no matter how long it takes for you to get your bearings. And while there may be some seasons of life where we struggle with this more than others, we can – each time we falter – use tools borrowed from DBT (specifically, chain and solution analyses; Linehan, 2015; Rizvi, 2019) to help us make progress in this regard. These evidenced-based, step-by-step processes can help us identify the links in the chain of events that led to a specific problematic behavior (e.g., yelling at our kids), thereby providing clues as to how we might break these links in order to reduce the likelihood that we'll repeat this behavior in the future.

Needless to say, taking time to own and examine our missteps can be incredibly painful and may even seem counterintuitive, especially for those of us who try to focus on the positive, rather than dwell on the negative. Understandably, most of us would prefer to just sweep the mistakes we make with our kids under the rug and pretend as though the hurtful things we said and did never happened. Unfortunately, although doing so may feel better for us in the moment, it practically guarantees that we'll stumble again in the future in the very same ways, if not more so. After all, we can't really change a behavior unless we first acknowledge the behavior and try to understand it. More specifically, we need to uncover the behavior's purpose or function (i.e., how it's serving us), as well as the factors that give rise to it. We also need to come up with alternative solutions to try the next time we find ourselves in a similar situation. Hence the need for these skills.

Conducting a Chain Analysis

Although the step-by-step guide that follows may seem overwhelming at first glance, I promise it's actually not all that complicated. If it helps, you can think of a chain analysis as a detailed story of how things went down. You can even imagine that you are a playwright, providing the same kind of fine-grained account that a director would need in order to bring your play to life. The only difference is that instead of using this information to create or replicate a scene, it will later be used to conduct a solution analysis in order to reduce the likelihood that a similarly thorny episode will occur again. With that in mind, here are the steps, each of which I've annotated with responses of my own from the filthy puddle story I shared in Chapter 1 in order to illustrate what this process looks like in practice:

1) First, we need to **identify and describe the problematic behavior**. What, specifically, did we do or say that we'd rather not do again? The goal here is to be as detailed and concrete as possible.

   - Although I engaged in many problematic behaviors that day (each of which could be examined with separate chain analyses), the first glare that I gave my daughter was what initially escalated the situation, so let's zoom in on this, specifically. (Note: simply saying that I was "mean" to my daughter wouldn't be sufficient here.)

2) Next, what was the **prompting event** that kicked off the chain leading to the problematic behavior?

   - My daughter intentionally shoved my son into a puddle of – let's be real – feces-laced mud (although I hadn't yet realized we were dealing with more than just mud).

3) What factors, both within and outside of you, made you especially **vulnerable** to the prompting event?

   - I was pretty much running on empty the day this happened. Due to the pandemic, I had been overworking myself for months, caring for my kids during the day and seeing patients late into the night, thereby leaving me sleep deprived on most days. It was also really hot and humid that day, so I was physically uncomfortable from the very moment we got to the park. Plus, my kids had done a good amount of whining, complaining, and limit-testing when we first got there, leaving me feeling a little more on edge than usual.

4) What **thoughts, feelings, behaviors, body sensations, or events** immediately followed the prompting event? What thoughts, feelings, behaviors, body sensations, or events came next? What happened after that? And after that? You get the idea. Keep going, adding as many links to the chain of events as you can recall leading up to the problematic behavior identified in Step 1. Figure 8.1 depicts the links connecting the shove my daughter gave her brother to the first glare I directed her way.

5) Next, what were the short- and long-term consequences of the problematic behavior for you and others? How did the problematic behavior make you and others feel and act, both in the moment and afterward? What, if any, effect did the problematic behavior have on your environment?

   - In the short term, it felt satisfying to act on the urge to glare at my daughter because I was so angry. However, glaring at her immediately dysregulated both of us even further.

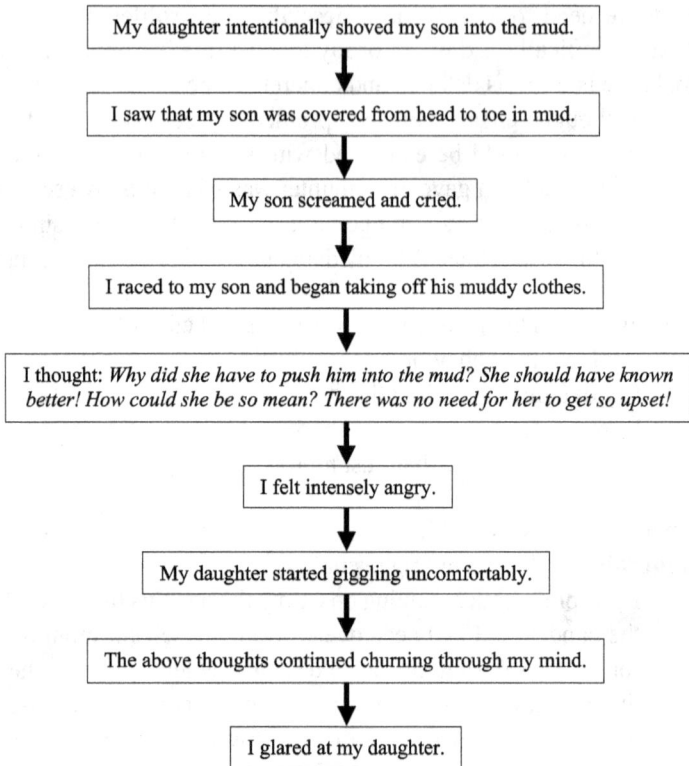

Figure 8.1 Example links in a chain analysis.

- More specifically, this glare fueled my anger, which later led to me speaking to both of my kids in a harsh and cold manner. Further, once my anger came down a bit, I was left feeling a tremendous amount of shame and guilt for how I had behaved.
- Additionally, glaring at my daughter likely left her feeling uneasy (and maybe even afraid of me), making it impossible for her to regulate and resist her urge to wipe "mud" all over our dog shortly thereafter.
- In the longer term, glaring at my daughter likely hurt my relationship with her by poking holes in her belief that my love is unconditional.
  - (Thankfully, however, glaring at my daughter didn't harm anyone else. Having said that, because it fueled my anger, glaring at her could have indirectly caused a collision had I given in to my angry urges to slam on my car's brakes when we were driving home later that day.)

And there you have it: the five steps to conducting a chain analysis. Although with practice, you may eventually be able to walk through a chain analysis in your head, I recommend writing your answers to the prompts for each of these steps when first using this skill. Whichever method you choose, Table 8.1 gives a quick breakdown of the process for you to refer back to as needed.

Table 8.1 Steps for conducting a chain analysis.

---

1) Define the problematic behavior. Be specific.
2) Define the prompting event.
3) Identify vulnerability factors.
4) Describe the chain of events linking the prompting event to the problematic behavior. Include all thoughts, feelings, behaviors, body sensations, and events.
5) Identify the short- and long-term consequences of the problematic behavior for you, others, and the environment.

Again, since I engaged in many problematic behaviors that day, I could also conduct separate chain analyses for each of these behaviors. However, now that you know how to use this tool, let's move on to the skill that always complements and follows a chain analysis.

Conducting a Solution Analysis

Once you've conducted a behavioral chain analysis, it's time to move on to conducting a solution analysis. Here are the steps:

1) Go back to the chain of events and identify points where you could have behaved differently. What skills could you have used to break these links? For those of you who are sports fans, this is your chance to Monday morning quarterback. Having said that, keep in mind that hindsight is 20/20 and that it's important to approach these next few steps non-judgmentally and with curiosity, creativity, and openness. In other words, this isn't about "should-ing" all over yourself, but rather compassionately giving yourself a mental do-over.
    - Upon reflection, any of the following skills would have likely helped me break the chain of events sooner, thereby eliminating the problematic behavior of glaring at my daughter (as well as the other problematic behaviors that followed).
        - **Reframe Unhelpful Thoughts** – Each time I had unhelpful thoughts about my daughter, I could have reframed

these thoughts. Specifically, I could have reminded myself that this was a hard day for her, too. Like me, she was hot, tired, and upset about the fact that her brother accidentally bumped into her, causing her to get mud in her boots. However, unlike me, she was working with an immature executive center that was not yet capable of inhibiting the strong urges her emotions were pulling for. Given this, I could have told myself something along the following lines: *She's clearly been hijacked by her emotions and needs help, not censure.*

- **Practice Opposite Action** – Instead of acting on my angry urges to glare at my daughter (and later speak harshly to her), I could have practiced opposite action by looking at her with kind eyes and speaking to her in a calm and gentle tone. I could have even told her that I love her and would be there to help her.
- **Practice Mindfulness** – Instead of stewing in my angry thoughts, I could have mindfully observed our beautiful surroundings (if you remember, we were at a lovely state park) or my own intense emotions. I could have even mindfully noticed my thoughts, which may have helped me get some distance from them and recognize them as thoughts, not facts. Alternatively, I could have mindfully observed my daughter, which may have helped me see that she was struggling and in need of help.
- **Use the CARE Skills** – Although I didn't have ice or ice water with me (oh, how I wish I did that day!) and likely couldn't have activated my body with exercise beyond our hot and weighty walk back to the car (which only amplified my emotions), I could have relaxed my muscles using progressive muscle relaxation or exhaled slowly in order to calm my breathing.

2) Next, consider what, if anything, you could have done to make yourself less vulnerable to the prompting event in the first place.
   - Because of the pandemic, there really wasn't all that much I could have done to ameliorate the burnout I was experiencing that day. The many balls that I was juggling at the time had pretty much depleted me, and yet, because of the pandemic, I couldn't outsource in the way that I otherwise might have in order to recharge. Getting help with childcare was not an option, and my husband was working long hours in the hospital. I also couldn't bring myself to drop my clinical work as I knew that my patients needed me due to the inordinate, pandemic-related stress they were also experiencing.

- Having said that, I certainly could have done some small things to make me less vulnerable that day, which may have enabled me to inhibit my urge to glare at my daughter after she pushed her brother into the filthy puddle.

  - For instance, I could have chosen to find a way to see patients during the day instead of at night. This would have left me with some time to recharge in the evenings and would have also enabled me to get more sleep.

  - In addition, I could have carved out more time for exercise in the days leading up to this, as it had been months (largely due to the pandemic) since I had really worked out.

  - Also, given that my daughter had chosen to dress much too warmly for the hot summer weather, I could have brought a change of clothes for her with us. Had I done so, she likely wouldn't have been quite so hot that day, which may have left her less emotionally vulnerable.

  - Relatedly, I could have brought wet wipes for cleaning up messes and an empty plastic bag for storing any discarded (or contaminated) items, which may have made the mess we found ourselves in seem at least a little less overwhelming.

3) Finally, what could you do the next time you find yourself faced with a similar prompting event? What skills could you use to prevent a recurrence of the problematic behavior? Once identified, commit to using these skills in the future in order to reduce the likelihood of deviating from behaving in a calm and connected manner moving forward. You may even opt to put some signs in key locations (e.g., on the lock screen of your phone, on your refrigerator door, and in your car), reminding you to use these skills in the future.

   - Forever seared in my brain, this incident has, in many ways, been a blessing for me as it has helped me see the importance of reducing vulnerability factors and using the other ART (Accept, Regulate, and Tolerate) Tools in order to prevent something similar (or worse) from happening again. Although I don't have any reminders of this posted anywhere, I no longer see patients at night, mostly to ensure that I have some time to myself in the evenings and can get to bed at a reasonable hour. I also regularly practice using these skills when I'm *not* emotionally charged as I find that doing so increases the likelihood that I'll use them in future challenging moments. And for moments when I do become emotionally flooded, I typically first turn to mindfulness, opposite action, and/or the CARE skills and then aim to reframe whatever unhelpful thoughts happen to be fueling my distress.

And that's it: the three steps to conducting a solution analysis. Once again, I recommend walking through each of these steps with pen and paper, especially when first using this skill, although you can certainly try going through this process in your head if and when you feel ready to do so. In case it helps, here's a quick overview of these steps for you to refer back to as needed (Table 8.2).

Table 8.2 Steps for conducting a solution analysis.

1) Identify skills that could have broken some of the links in the chain of events.
2) Identify steps you could have taken to make you less vulnerable to the prompting event.
3) Create a plan to use the next time you find yourself in a similar situation.

Repairing and Getting Back on Track

If you take nothing else from this book, I hope you'll remember the following: Mess-ups are bound to happen when caring for children, but these don't make you a bad parent or spell doom for your kids or your relationships with them. To the contrary, modeling problem-solving by conducting chain and solution analyses in order to change our own unhelpful patterns can be incredibly powerful for our children to see and teaches them that it's okay to not be perfect. Likewise, repairing any rifts that we cause or contribute to by offering genuine apologies for our actions can help soothe us and our children and demonstrates for our kids how to acknowledge and make amends for our mistakes, thereby empowering them to one day do the same. I truly can't think of a better gift we could give them.

Having said that, let's talk about what an effective apology entails, even though I realize this may seem unnecessary to some. For those who might find it helpful, the acronym ASAP can be used to remember the four most important components. Expounded upon in the following paragraphs, they are:

Authenticity
Specificity
Accountability
Prevention

First, **authenticity** is key. If you are apologizing but not really feeling sorry for your actions, chances are your kids will read through this, making your words ring hollow. Second is **specificity**. Saying "I'm sorry" or "I'm sorry I upset you" without acknowledging the specific behavior(s) you wish you hadn't engaged in doesn't mean all that much.

Third, and equally important, is taking **accountability** for the problematic behavior(s), without trying to blame the other person for our missteps. For instance, when apologizing to my daughter after the filthy puddle incident we just chained together, I made sure to fully own my actions. Instead of saying, "I'm sorry I glared at you and spoke in such a cold and harsh voice today, but you shouldn't have pushed your brother into the mud or covered Yogi with it," I said, "I'm sorry I glared at you and spoke in such a cold and harsh voice today. I was upset seeing your brother and Yogi covered in that yucky mud, but you never deserve to be treated like that." Whereas responses such as the former essentially deflect all responsibility onto our kids, responses along the lines of the latter make it clear that the onus to stay calm rests with us, no matter the prompting event.

The final step is to articulate a **prevention** plan for how to reduce the likelihood that you'll repeat the problematic behavior(s) in the future, enlisting your kid's help, if needed. Here's where you can note the specific skills you identified that you intend to use the next time you find yourself feeling heated. You may also want to ask your child if there's anything you could do to help prevent a recurrence of the prompting event, while letting them know that regardless of whether the prompting event happens again, you're going to aim to use the tools identified to help you keep your cool. To round out the prior example, here's the gist of the prevention plan I shared with my daughter after we had both cooled off:

> The next time we find ourselves in a tricky situation, I'm going to take some slow breaths and do the opposite of what my anger wants me to do so that I can support you without glaring at you or speaking in an unkind way. I'm also going to try to sleep and exercise more going forward, as I tend to be less likely to lose my cool when I'm well rested and have had a chance to move my body.

Of course, even with the best of plans and intentions, we will likely trip up when with our kids in similar and different ways time and again. Each time we do, we can come back to these same steps: 1) conduct a chain analysis to dissect what happened; 2) conduct a solution analysis to identify ways we might be more skillful down the road; and 3) use the acronym

ASAP (Authenticity, Specificity, Accountability, Prevention) to apologize and repair with our children. Although certainly easier said than done, this kind of honest reflection and vulnerability is the glue of healthy relationships, whether with our kids or anyone else.

Further, aside from helping us maintain strong bonds with our children, following these steps can have an enormous impact on whether and how our kids atone for mistakes themselves. Indeed, as both research and lived experience suggest, our kids learn so many vital life skills, including how to give an effective apology, simply by watching us (van der Storm et al., 2021). As I told Jake, I've never once insisted that my kids apologize to me or anyone else, and yet my kids have become experts in offering sincere apologies. Without any formal instruction from me or my husband – only many observations of us apologizing to them, each other, and others – my kids have learned how to deliver more meaningful apologies than most adults I know. And before they were ready to make these kinds of repairs themselves, I would (as I instructed Jake) do so for them, apologizing to whomever they hurt or upset while noting the specific steps I planned to take to prevent a recurrence of the problematic behavior(s). Occasionally, I'd let my kids know that the affected individual(s) might appreciate an apology, but the choice as to whether or not to give one was and has always been up to them.

Where to Go From Here?

Even after a successful repair, how to proceed may not always be clear. Maybe our confidence has been shaken and we're scared of repeating our mistakes. Maybe we're afraid that our kids aren't developing as they should. Or maybe a palpable sense of detachment is continuing to linger in the air, whether driven by us, our kids, or both. Whatever's obscuring the way forward, we can find our way by letting connection be our North Star and continuing from there. Remember, connection comes in many forms. Maybe we take our kids on a special outing, offer to play a favorite game with them, or give them extra snuggles at bedtime. Maybe we simply observe them at play or work. Or maybe we sit with them as they vent about how unfair life is or cry in our arms. However we choose to proceed, reading the room and using mindful acceptance as our springboard to connection is all that's really needed. After all, it's hard to not feel connected when we're accepted exactly as we are.

Trust Development

This brings us to one of my final parting messages: Trust development. If your kids aren't yet able to do things you believe they should be able to do or if they're engaging in behaviors you think they should have already outgrown, rest assured that this likely won't always be the case. After all, even if your kid is the last one in his class to still wear diapers, chances are you won't be sending him off to college in pull-ups. Although it's normal and natural to want to rush our kids to certain milestones or through challenging phases, doing so rarely strengthens our relationships with them. Instead, when we act on urges to speed things along, we – knowingly or unknowingly – send the message that we don't fully accept our kids as they are, thereby weakening our connections with them. To be sure, our kids may sometimes need extra support to help them acquire skills that their same-age peers already have. For example, your kid may benefit from having an aide in the classroom to help him stay on task. Yet, even when this is the case, we can still convey acceptance of exactly where our kids are at any given moment in time, knowing that in doing so, we're not only strengthening our connections with them but also giving them a sizable leg up to getting wherever it is we hope they'll one day go.

One thing that helps me sometimes in this regard is to imagine that my children are artists who've been commissioned to create masterpieces of their choosing. Although their pieces will be works in progress for the remainder of their lives, I have the honor and privilege of taking in the beauty (and sometimes mess) that's already on their canvasses and witnessing their creative process unfold minute by minute, day by day. Sure, I'm allowed to give some input, but ultimately, what they paint and how they go about painting is really up to them. Whenever possible, I try to trust their process and resist the urge to rush their paintings along or interfere with their creative vision in any way. Aside from being less stressful for me, choosing to observe instead of critique or direct allows my kids to express themselves more fully and authentically through their work. They also clearly enjoy their jobs much more when I'm not nagging them every minute but am instead giving them space to create as they see fit.

Be Kind to Yourself

Though the journeys we are on as parents will certainly never be easy, my hope is that the perspectives, anecdotes, and skills shared throughout these pages will enable you to move more gracefully through the ups and downs of parenthood. Whether your children are infants, toddlers, tweens, teenagers, young adults, or somewhere in between, I encourage you to reach for the ART Tools as often as possible to help you accept, regulate, and tolerate your emotions, keeping in mind that the more you practice, the more natural and automatic using these skills will become. Although none of these tools will ever be universally effective, the more familiar we become with each of them, the greater the odds that we'll eventually come to intuitively select those tools most appropriate for a given moment. Further, while these skills will hopefully enable you to experience parenthood as more enjoyable and fulfilling, remember that even the most mundane, annoying, and infuriating of circumstances with our kids can take on new meaning if we can remember to view these instances as golden invitations to use our tools, rather than as moments to dread and avoid at all costs.

Having said that, I want to stress one final time that you are not expected to be skillful every second with your kids. Please be kind to yourself on days when you aren't your best and see these as opportunities for learning, rather than evidence that you are failing as a parent. Let each stumble be a reminder to return to this book and the skills within it, as well as a reminder to be gentle with yourself as you continue striving to relate differently to the emotions within and outside of you. Change rarely comes in one fell swoop and is often experienced as one step forward and two steps backward. All that matters is that you keep trying to move ahead, no matter how many times you falter. Whether with chocolate, a bubble bath, a dance party, or just a high five, celebrate each step you take toward being the calm and connected parent you aspire to be, keeping in mind that it's okay to be generous when identifying these wins. In fact, now that you've managed to make it to the end of this book, I encourage you to celebrate this very moment in whatever way feels best for you.

But first, let me congratulate you on becoming the newest member of the Emotion-Savvy Parenting Club. Welcome! I'm so glad we're in this together.

References

Casey, B. J., Jones, R. M., & Hare, T. A. (2008). The adolescent brain. *Annals of the New York Academy of Sciences, 1124*, 111–126. https://doi.org/10.1196/annals.1440.010

Linehan, M. M. (2015). *DBT skills training manual* (2nd ed.). The Guilford Press.

Loewen Nair, A. (2016, September 1). *7 ways to help your child handle their "after school restraint collapse"* [Blog post]. https://www.yummymummyclub.ca/blogs/andrea-nair-connect-four-parenting/20160830/after-school-restraint-collapse-help-your-child

Rizvi, S. L. (2019). *Chain analysis in dialectical behavior therapy.* The Guilford Press.

van der Storm, L., van Lissa, C. J., Lucassen, N., Helmerhorst, K. O. W., & Keizer, R. (2021). Maternal and paternal parenting and child prosocial behavior: A meta-analysis using a structural equation modeling design. *Marriage & Family Review, 58*(1), 1–37. https://doi.org/10.1080/01494929.2021.1927931

Index

Note: Page numbers in *italics* indicate figures; page numbers in **bold** indicate tables.

For Product Safety Concerns and Information please contact our EU
representative GPSR@taylorandfrancis.com
Taylor & Francis Verlag GmbH, Kaufingerstraße 24, 80331 München, Germany

www.ingramcontent.com/pod-product-compliance
Lightning Source LLC
Chambersburg PA
CBHW071745270326
41928CB00013B/2798